The Only Basic Piano INSTRUCTION BOOK YOU'LL EVER NEED

The Only Basic Piano

INSTRUCTION BOOK · YOU'LL EVER NEED

Learn to Play—from Reading Your First Notes to Constructing Complex Chords

BROOKE HALPIN

Adams Media
Avon, Massachusetts

Published by Adams Media, a division of F+W Media, Inc., 57 Littlefield Street, Avon, MA 02322. U.S.A.
www.adamsmedia.com

ISBN-13: 978-1-59337-380-1   Printed in Canada.   J I H G F E D C
ISBN-10: 1-59337-380-5
Library of Congress Cataloging-in-Publication Data available from publisher.

This book is available at quantity discounts for bulk purchases.
For information, please call 1-800-289-0963.

CONTENTS

Introduction

Ray Charles. Elton John. Vladimir Horowitz. Billy Joel. You.

Question: What do these five people have in common?
Answer: All of them, at one point in their lives, didn't know how to play the piano.

It's true, you *still* don't know how to play the piano, or at least play more than a little, and everyone else on the list eventually went far past that point. But even Mozart had to start somewhere. (Of course, he had the advantage of starting by age three.)

Listening to the glorious music of your piano heroes can be inspiring—it's no doubt part of what inspired you to pick up this book—but also daunting. More so than with any other instrument, the way that ten fingers can use a piano to create a cascade of musical sound can seem miraculous, and beyond the capability of someone without remarkable talent. This can be true even if you have limited goals. You aren't trying to race through a Beethoven sonata at breakneck speed like Horowitz, but you'd like to know how to play a simple Bach prelude. You don't hope to tour the world as a famous singer-songwriter; you'd be happy to play "Just the Way You Are" in your living room.

The important thing to remember is this: You have what it takes. You have that piano in the family room that you've been meaning to play, or you have the willingness to go out and find the right piano to buy or rent. You have an appreciation for the music a piano can make, and the desire to create some of it yourself. And you have *The Only Basic Piano Instruction Book You'll Ever Need.* Put it all together, along with some dedicated practice time, and you *will* be able to achieve at least some of your piano-playing dreams.

In this book, you'll start with the basics of selecting and caring for a piano, learn what you need to know about music terminology and notation, and begin to play the piano—first with your right hand, then your left, and finally with both. Later chapters will explore the mysteries of key signatures, sharps, flats, chords, and more. Along the way, you'll do exercises—eighty in all—that make the concepts clear and gradually develop your abilities. There may be times when your new second language of music is hard to understand (root position? enharmonic equivalents?), and when your own progress is hard to see. Don't worry. Just take a deep breath, and go back through the exercise or that section of a chapter one more time. And keep playing.

one

**How to Choose and
Care for Your Piano**

BUYING A PIANO can be a major decision financially, and learning to play one takes a significant investment of your time. Before you rush off to purchase an impressive grand piano that's too big for your budget and your living room, or a worn-out upright that's quite cheap (but, unfortunately, unplayable), consider the following advice on how to select and care for the piano that's just right for you.

Before You Go Shopping for a Piano

You should first determine which room in your home or apartment is best suited to accommodate a piano. (You should try, for example, to place the piano far away from the television.) For the professional musician who spends a lot of time playing the piano, it might be best to put the piano in a spare room or guest bedroom.

Next, figure out how much money you are willing to spend. If you have a big apartment or home and really want a grand piano but have a small budget, you can make a down payment and finance the remaining balance.

What you're willing to pay for a piano will also determine whether you buy a new or used piano. New pianos are generally more expensive than used or restored pianos. An exception would be a rare restored piano, which might cost considerably more than a new piano.

Settle on a Size and Style

What you can afford to spend, along with the space you have available, will usually determine the size of the piano. The most affordable pianos are *spinets* and *consoles*, which are the smallest acoustic pianos made. Spinets are good for beginners, but very few piano manufacturers make new spinets. Consoles are the next size up and cost a little more than spinets. *Studio* pianos are even bigger in size and price. *Upright* pianos are taller and more expensive than studios.

All of the above varieties are vertical pianos, meaning that the soundboard and the piano strings are placed vertically. *Grand* pianos, which are the most expensive, have strings that run horizontally. They range in size from petite (or baby) grands to concert grands.

All types of pianos come in a variety of finishes, including high-gloss black, satin black, cherry, mahogany, walnut, or oak. The style of the casing also has several varieties, including modern, French Provincial, Italian

Provincial, Queen Anne, and Louis XVI. You want to choose a piano that blends in with the overall style and design of the room you're going to put it in.

Most of the pianos that you might buy are made in the United States, Germany, or Asia. The primary U.S. manufacturers are Baldwin and Steinway, and to a smaller extent, Mason & Hamlin and Charles R. Walter. Steinway also makes pianos in Germany, which tend to be more expensive than their American models. Other German manufacturers include Blüthner, Bechstein, Grotrian, Schimmel, and Seiler. Asian manufacturers include Kawai, Knabe, Samick, Yamaha, and Young Chang.

New or Used?

Prices of pianos can vary greatly depending on the different types of sizes, cabinets, and finishes. With new pianos, prices start as low as around $3,000 for a small vertical piano; prices for a 9-foot concert grand can go above $100,000.

Used pianos come in all sizes and models, with the exception of limited custom editions and rare pianos, which are hard to find and are generally quite expensive. There are two basic categories of used pianos: "as is" and rebuilt or restored. "As is" pianos, more often than not, need to be rebuilt, at least to some extent. Some "as is" pianos need to be completely restored, which can be quite costly, and in some cases even more expensive than buying a new piano.

Piano prices for used verticals at retail outlets can start as low as $1,000 and go as high as $5,000, depending on the manufacturer, model, and condition of the piano. Used grand piano prices can start as low as $2,500 and go as high as $35,000. Here again, the difference in price depends on the manufacturer, model, and condition of the piano.

If you're going to buy a used or restored piano, be prepared to ask the salesperson a lot of questions, such as:

- When was the piano built?
- What is the condition of the soundboard? Has it been replaced?
- Have the strings, felts, hammers, and action been replaced?

- Under normal playing conditions, how long will the piano last?
- Other than the difference in price, why should I buy a used piano instead of a new piano?

Another thing you should do when looking for a used piano is to get in touch with your local music schools or the music department of a community college or university. Periodically, these places replace their old pianos with new ones, and this presents an excellent opportunity to get a used piano at a very good price.

Acoustic or Digital?

Many people—particularly those with a lower budget for a piano or a smaller home to put one in—are now choosing to buy a digital piano instead of a traditional acoustic one. A digital piano is an electric keyboard that produces sound through prerecorded sampled sounds (usually from an acoustic piano) that are amplified through speakers.

Digital pianos—from such makers as Roland, Yamaha, and Casio—range in price from an extreme low of $500 to around $1,500 or more for a better-quality instrument. The keys of a digital piano have a weighted key action that imitates the action of acoustic pianos. When evaluating a digital piano, pay special attention to how closely the action feels like that of an acoustic piano. You should also make sure that the piano has a full complement of 88 keys, as some lower-priced models do not.

Some advantages of a digital piano over an acoustic one:

1. They are portable and weigh much less than acoustic pianos.
2. They don't need to be tuned, as the digital sounds are stored on microprocessing chips.
3. They can be played silently through headphones. This is a good option to have for beginning piano players in particular, who may not want to disturb other household members.
4. Most digital pianos have a MIDI interface, which allows them to connect with other MIDI instruments or with a computer.
5. You can usually record what you have played, either through an output jack onto a tape, or by using a special feature included with the piano.
6. Most digital pianos can switch to other "voices" at the push of a button, such as the sounds of an organ, harpsichord, or electric piano.

Disadvantages of digital pianos include:

1. Although the technology behind digital pianos is constantly improving, the sound quality still does not equal that of acoustic pianos.
2. The recorded sound samples are set and cannot be enhanced or colored by the subtle playing ability of the pianist in the same way as with an acoustic piano. This is particularly true in the case of dynamics, which relates to the loudness or softness of notes.
3. Many digital piano models have limited polyphony, which is the ability to play a number of keys simultaneously.
4. Some digital pianos are available with attractive cases and stands, but they still are not the impressive and beautiful objects that many traditional pianos are.

One possibility for a beginning player is to buy or rent a digital piano at first (especially when cost, space, and portability are paramount considerations), and then later switch to an acoustic piano, as you become more confident in your playing ability and in your long-term commitment to having a piano in your home.

Making Your Final Decision

Narrow your choices down to two or three pianos. If you can, play the same piece of music on each one and make comparisons. Which one sounds better? Which one is easier to play? Which one feels better? Ask the salesperson to tell you the differences and the pros and cons of each piano.

If you're still undecided and you have a friend or family member who plays the piano, ask him or her to go to the piano store with you and play the pianos you are considering. Ask for his or her opinion.

It's always a good idea to shop around and not limit your potential purchase to one piano store or retail outlet. By doing so, you'll get an excellent education, which will help you in your decision-making process. Also, don't feel as though you have to pay the asking price. Every piano store wants your business, so you can say it's a buyer's market when it comes to pianos. You can negotiate with the salesperson and make a counteroffer.

Taking Care of Your Piano

A piano functions best under consistent climatic conditions—not too moist or too dry. The ideal temperature is 68 degrees with 42 percent relative humidity.

Pianos are primarily made of wood. Changes in humidity cause the wooden parts of a piano to swell and shrink, and these changes have a direct impact on the tuning and action of pianos. When extreme swings occur in humidity levels, wood can crack and glue joints can be damaged.

Hundreds of felt and leather parts in the piano's action are also affected by changes in humidity, which can increase friction and make the piano's action feel stiff and resistant to the touch. Under conditions of very high humidity, condensation can build up on the metal parts of the piano and eventually rust the strings, tuning pins, and iron plate.

The opposite extreme is having a piano in a very dry climate. A climate that is very arid can dry out the wooden parts of the piano and cause them to crack.

When your piano is kept at a constant moisture level, shrinking and swelling are minimized, and your piano will stay in tune for a longer period of time. The best way to maintain a consistent humidity level is to install a humidity control system. This device, which can be attached directly to a piano, has three parts: a humidifier that adds moisture, a dehumidifier that eliminates excessive moisture, and a humidistat that detects the relative humidity of the air within the piano and adds or removes moisture as needed.

You should also beware of direct sunlight. Do not place your piano in front of windows or below skylights. The ultraviolet rays of the sun can damage the finish on your piano. With repeated exposure to the sun, the piano casing will get bleached out, blisters may appear on the finish, and the piano may go out of tune.

Keeping Your Piano in Tune

If you protect your piano from direct sunlight, excessive moisture, and extreme dryness, your piano is more likely to stay in tune. But even under the best conditions, pianos still need to be tuned at least once a year. Depending on how critical your ears are, and the age and condition of your piano, you may need to tune your piano every six months.

If you reposition your piano in your home, it probably won't need to be tuned after moving it. However, when a piano is moved to a different home, it will more than likely need to be tuned once it reaches its new location.

For the courageous individual who has very good ears, you might want to get a tuning hammer and tune a string or two. But you could do more harm than good. The overall tuning of the piano involves all of the strings. When attempting to tune a note that sounds either sharp or flat, you could be dealing with a note that has two or three strings. You have to be able to isolate the string that sounds out of tune and match it with the other string or strings. This requires the use of a rubber insert to stop the other string or strings from resonating. You also have to compare the string with its upper and lower octaves. It is far better to have an experienced piano technician tune your piano.

Piano Note

Every piano is different. The sound, feel, and action of a piano are based on your own subjectivity. Granted, most ears can hear the qualities that are inherent in high-quality pianos, which sound better than pianos of a lesser quality. However, what sounds or feels good to one person might not be the same for another. Therefore, you have to spend some time with each piano you are thinking of buying.

two

Learning
the Basics

NOW THAT YOU HAVE A PIANO, you are no doubt anxious to play it. In this chapter, you'll learn about the musical language and symbols you'll need to know throughout your piano studies. You'll then begin playing some basic exercises, working your way up to a simple little tune.

The Language of Music

Anyone can listen to music. However, the making and playing of music requires more than listening. It requires the know-how. If you want to play the piano, you're going to have to study, take lessons, and practice.

In order to understand the discussions and exercises throughout this book, you will need to know some of the basic terms used in music and their definitions.

Bar lines—Bar lines are placed between measures. In 4/4 time, a bar line is placed after the fourth beat of each measure.

Bass line—The bass line, played by the left hand, accompanies the melody. Bass lines usually play the root of the chord and can also include the fifth and third of the chord and passing tones.

Beat—A beat is a measurement of time. For example, in a 4/4 time signature, there are four beats in a measure of music. The beats in music help you keep even time.

Chords—Basic chords are comprised of three notes: the root, the third, and the fifth. Three-note chords are called triads.

Clefs—There are three clefs in music: treble, tenor, and bass clefs. In piano music, the treble and bass clefs are used. The treble clef is also called the G clef; the bass clef is also called the F clef. Clefs sit at the far left end of a staff and determine the letter names of the notes.

Harmony—Usually comprised of chords, harmony supports the melody. In piano music, the harmony is generally played with the left hand.

Key signature—The key signature tells you what key a piece of music is written in. There are two kinds of key signatures: sharp (♯) and flat (♭). The key signature is written on the staff to the immediate right of the clef.

Ledger lines—These are short horizontal lines found above and below the five lines of the staff. Ledger lines accommodate notes that are above G at the top of the staff and below D at the bottom of the staff. For instance, middle C on your keyboard is written on one ledger line below the staff.

Measure/Bar—A measure of music is the same as a bar of music. A measure, or bar, contains a number of beats, as designated by the time signature. For instance, when the time signature is 4/4, there are four beats per measure.

Melody—Melody is the dominant musical line that is usually played by the right hand on the piano and is usually written in the treble clef.

Notes—Musical notes are used to determine the duration and value of the note being played. Notes and their values are: whole notes, half notes, quarter notes, eighth notes, sixteenth notes, and thirty-second notes.

Pitch—Pitch is determined by where the note is played on the piano and its corresponding written note on manuscript paper.

Rests—Rests represent silence in music. When you see a rest, stop playing for the duration and value of what the rest is equal to. There are whole rests, half rests, quarter rests, eighth rests, sixteenth rests, and thirty-second rests. Rests are of equal value to notes. For instance, a quarter rest is equal in value to a quarter note, which represents one beat.

Rhythm—Rhythm occurs when playing a series of notes.

Staff—Staffs are made up of horizontal lines and spaces. When using a treble clef, the lines on a staff from bottom to top are: E, G, B, D, and F. To help remember these letter names to the corresponding lines, think of this saying: "Every Good Boy Does Fine." The letter names of the spaces on the staff between the lines are: F, A, C, and E. When you put the letter names of the lines and spaces together, you get E, F, G, A, B, C, D, E, and F, which correspond directly with letter names of the piano keys.

Stems—Stems are attached to notes. There are quarter-note stems, eighth-note stems, sixteenth-note stems, and thirty-second–note stems.

Tempo—The tempo is the rate of speed at which you're playing music.

Time signature—The time signature tells you how many beats there are per measure.

Now that you have the terminology down, you are ready to begin your first lesson. The following series of exercises are written for the beginner level. As the chapters and exercises in this book progress, they reach a more intermediate level.

The Notes on the Keyboard

Fig. A: Abbreviated keyboard

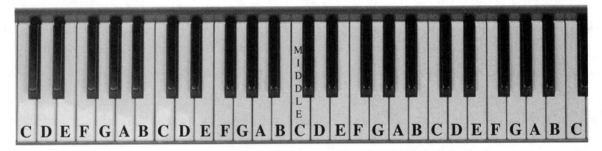

1. 2. 3. 4. 5. - the fingers of your right hand

The above illustration shows the center of the keyboard, not the full eighty-eight keys found on acoustic pianos. A full keyboard has an additional twenty-four keys above the far right C key and another fifteen keys below the far left C key. The additional keys follow the same white key/black key configuration. The highest note on an acoustic piano is C; the lowest note is A. As you can see in the illustration, the notes of the piano's white keys are C, D, E, F, G, A, and B. The notes of the black keys are C-sharp, D-sharp, F-sharp, G-sharp, and A-sharp.

The black keys are located between the white keys. They are grouped in sets of two and three. For instance, C-sharp and D-sharp make up a group of two black keys while F-sharp, G-sharp, and A-sharp make up a group of three. This two- and three-group black note sequence is consistent up and down the keyboard. The black keys are called sharp keys because they're slightly higher (sharper) than the white key that precedes it. For instance, the black key C-sharp is slightly higher in sound and pitch than the white key C. When playing in flat key signatures, the black keys are also called flat keys.

The note called middle C is located approximately in the middle of the keyboard. Actually, it's a little left of the middle; and if you count up from the lowest note on a keyboard instrument that has eighty-eight keys, middle C will be the fortieth note up from the bottom.

Putting Your Fingers on the Keys

Looking at your right hand, let's assign numbers to each of your fingers. Your thumb is 1, index finger is 2, middle finger is 3, forefinger (ring finger) is 4, and your smallest finger is 5. Take a look at **Fig. A** again, and let's assign corresponding numbers to the keys starting with middle C. C is 1 (your thumb), D is 2 (your index finger), E is 3 (your middle finger), F is 4 (your forefinger), and G is 5 (your smallest finger).

Two-Finger Exercise

This first series of exercises will use only your first two fingers: your thumb (1) and your index finger (2).

Place your thumb on middle C, press down on the key, and release it. Repeat this action a number of times. Place your index finger on the D key and do the same. Play D a number of times. Using your thumb to play middle C and your index finger to play D, alternate playing both notes in the following sequence: C, D, C, D, C. Try to play the two notes evenly with the same measured time for each note. Keep playing this simple two-finger exercise until it feels comfortable and sounds good.

Three-Finger Exercise

Now let's add your third (middle) finger to the exercise. Place your third finger over the E key (key 3) and press and release it a few times. With your thumb positioned above middle C, your second finger above D, and your third finger above E, play the following sequence of notes: C, E, D, E; C, E, D, E; C, E, D, E, C. Another way of thinking and playing this exercise is to use the corresponding number of your fingering sequence: 1, 3, 2, 3; 1, 3, 2, 3; 1, 3, 2, 3, 1 (1 represents your thumb, 3 represents your middle finger, 2 represents your index finger, 3 represents your middle finger).

The written music for this three-finger exercise looks like this:

Exercise 1: Three-finger exercise

Fingers: 1 3 2 3   1 3 2 3   1 3 2 3   1

C E D E   C E D E   C E D E   C

It's important to note that the middle C on your keyboard corresponds to the written quarter note C, located on one ledger line below the staff. This note is the first written note in **Exercise 1**.

Now play this exercise reading the music. Your fingers and hand stay in the same position, so you don't have to look down at them. Instead, keep your eyes on the music. Keep repeating this exercise until it feels good and sounds good.

Fig. B: Abbreviated keyboard

Exercise #2 - Starting on D: 1. 2. 3. (first 3 fingers - right hand)
Exercise #3 - Starting on E: 1. 2. 3.
Exercise #4 - Starting on F: 1. 2. 3.
Exercise #5 - Starting on G: 1. 2. 3.
Exercise #6 - Starting on A: 1. 2. 3.
Exercise #7 - Starting on B: 1. 2. 3.
Exercise #8 - Starting on C: 1. 2. 3.

Using the same three fingers (the thumb, index finger, and middle finger), place your thumb above the D key, index finger above the E key, and your middle finger above the F key (see **Fig. B**). Play the following sequence of notes: D, F, E, F; D, F, E, F; D, F, E, F, D. The corresponding numbers of your fingering sequence is exactly the same as **Exercise 1**: 1, 3, 2, 3; 1, 3, 2, 3; 1, 3, 2, 3, 1 (1 represents your thumb, 3 represents your middle finger, 2 represents your index finger, 3 represents your middle finger).

The written music looks like this:

Exercise 2

Congratulations! You have just played the first in a series of sequential exercises. The fingering configuration—1, 3, 2, 3; 1, 3, 2, 3; 1, 3, 2, 3, 1—can be played on any group of three piano keys. For example, in **Exercise 1**, you played this configuration starting with your thumb on the C key. In **Exercise 2**, you played the same configuration starting with your thumb on the D key.

Understanding the Symbols

Before we continue with the exercises, let's take a close look at all the symbols used in **Exercise 2**.

First, we see a treble clef sitting on the far left of the staff. The treble clef is also called the G clef because the curl wraps around and stops at the G line on the staff. This clef tells you that the letter names of the lines and spaces on the staff are: E, F, G, A, B, C, D, E, and F.

Next, we see the first note D, which is a quarter note and whose value is one quarter beat in the measure. As you can see, the quarter note is shaped like a filled-in circle with a stem attached to it. The following F, E, and F are also quarter notes. So, we have four quarter notes (D, F, E, F) in the first measure.

Immediately following the fourth quarter note in the first measure is a bar line. The bar line separates the measures on the staff and keeps the four quarter notes together in one measure. The next measure (measure 2) is an exact repetition of measure 1: same notes, same keys, same fingering, and same number of beats in the measure. The same is true in measure 3—a direct repetition of measures 1 and 2. Again, please notice the bar lines separating each measure.

In measure 4 we see only one quarter note followed by a quarter rest (the curved zigzag line) and a half rest (the small rectangular block that sits on the middle line of the staff). A quarter rest equals a quarter beat, and a half rest equals two beats. The combined value of one quarter note, one quarter rest, and one half rest gives us four beats in measure 4. The first beat has sound, which is the quarter note D. The second beat is silent, represented by the quarter rest. And the third and fourth beats are silent, represented by the half rest.

The symbol we see at the very end of the staff is called a double bar line. The double bar line means this is the end of the piece.

Moving Around the Keyboard

Let's continue with the exercises using the same sequence starting on different notes.

As you can see in **Exercise 3** below, the fingering is exactly the same as **Exercises 1 and 2**. The only differences are the pitches and letter names of the notes. You're simply moving your first three fingers up the keyboard and playing the same sequence. Play **Exercise 3** starting with your thumb playing the E key, followed by your middle finger playing the G key, and your index finger playing the F key.

Exercise 3

As you play the exercises, try to play the quarter notes evenly, since they all have the same equal value.

If you get lost during the course of playing these exercises, refer to **Fig. B**. This illustration shows you where the letter names of the notes on the staff are relative to the piano keys. For instance, the first note in **Exercise 4** is F, which is four notes above middle C on your piano.

Play **Exercise 4** starting with your thumb playing the F key, followed by your middle finger playing the A key, etc.

Your hand and fingers should never be flat when playing the keyboard. Be sure to keep your right hand arched and your fingers curved when playing these exercises.

Exercise 4

Now try **Exercise 5**.

Exercise 5

17

Looks like there's something new in this exercise. Immediately following the treble clef are two fours, one on top of the other. This is a time signature. The top number four tells you there are four beats per measure, and the bottom number four represents the quarter note, telling you the quarter note gets the beat. **Exercises 1, 2, 3, and 4** are also in 4/4 time.

This time start the sequence on the A key.

Exercise 6

Something new has been added in **Exercise 6**. The word *moderato* in the upper left-hand corner indicates the rate of speed at which the exercise should be played. *Moderato* is an Italian word that means "moderately"— not too fast and not too slow. This is the tempo (rate of speed) at which the music is to be played.

The first note in **Exercise 7** is B.

Exercise 7

There is a change in the placement and direction of the quarter note stems in **Exercises 5, 6, and 7**. In the previous exercises, all of the quarter note stems are placed on the right side of the notes and go upward. When notes are on the middle line of the staff (B) and higher, note stems are placed on the left side of the note and go downward.

Directly below the 4/4 time signature is the symbol *mf*. This symbol stands for the Italian term *mezzo forte*, which in English means "medium loud." **Exercise 7** should be played at a moderate tempo and played medium loud.

Exercise 8 introduces another musical symbol called the repeat sign. It is located immediately to the right of the 4/4 time signature and again at the end of measure 4. As you can see, a repeat sign is a double bar line with two small circles in the A and C spaces of the staff. There is also written text telling you to repeat three times at the end of measure 4. This tells you that after you have played the exercise once, you are to repeat the entire exercise twice. In doing so, you will have played the exercise a total of three times.

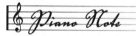

You should start playing each new exercise slowly. Once you have played the exercise correctly, then increase your tempo (speed) to moderato. If you get confused with your fingering, refer to **Figs. A and B** as needed.

Be sure to give the quarter rest and the half rest in measure 4 their full values totaling three beats of silence— one beat for the quarter rest, two beats for the half rest. It might help to count *one, two, three, four* for each beat per measure. For instance in measures 1, 2, and 3, as you're playing the quarter notes C, E, D, E, say *one, two, three, four*. When you get to measure 4, count *one* for the C note, *two* for the quarter rest, and *three, four* for the half rest.

Play **Exercise 8** starting with the C key.

Exercise 8

Moderato

(repeat 3 times)

1 3 2 3 1 3 2 3 1 3 2 3 1

mf C E D E C E D E C E D E C

Chapter Two: Learning the Basics

Understanding Octaves

There is a direct correlation between **Exercise 1** and **Exercise 8**: Both exercises have the same letter names for the notes—C, E, D, E; C, E, D, E; C, E, D, E; C. The difference is the placement of the notes on the staff and corresponding piano keys. The notes in **Exercise 8** are an octave higher than those in **Exercise 1**. *Octave* is a musical term referring to a pitch that is eight notes above a note that has the same letter name.

Place your thumb on middle C (the first note in **Exercise 1**, written on one ledger line below the staff) and count the keys moving up the keyboard until you reach the C (the first note in **Exercise 8**, written in the third space of the staff). The high C is exactly eight white keys higher than middle C, thus an octave higher.

Using these two Cs as a model, do the same with the second note E in **Exercise 1** and the second note E in **Exercise 8**. You will discover that there are the same number of white keys from the E on the first line of the staff in **Exercise 1** to the higher E in the fourth space on the staff in **Exercise 8**. Now do the same comparison with the third note D in both **Exercises 1 and 8**, and you will discover the same thing: There are eight white keys from the low D to the high D.

Playing Your First Simple Tune

Now that you have played the first eight exercises, it's time to play your first piece of music. This little tune is comprised of sections from **Exercises 1, 2, and 3**. As you can see, the fingering of the right hand is not indicated beyond measure 4. This is because the fingering pattern is already established and keeps repeating throughout the piece (1, 3, 2, 3, 1).

As the time signature indicates, there are four beats per measure. Be sure to give all the measures their full four beats, including the measures that have rests.

Let's take a closer look at **Exercise 9**. This piece is written using a two-bar pattern. The two-bar pattern is a series of four quarter notes in the first measure followed by one quarter note, one quarter rest, and a half rest in the second measure. This is a rhythmic pattern—it creates a specific rhythm that is repeated throughout the piece. The rhythm of the pattern is the same; however, the pitches change. In measures 1 and 2, the pitches are C, E, D, E, C. In measures 3 and 4, the pitches rise to D, F, E, F, D. In measures 5 and 6, the pitches rise to E, G, F, G, E. Measures 7 and 8 are exactly the same as measures 3 and 4. And measures 9 and 10 are exactly the same as measures 1 and 2.

Exercise 9

NICE and EASY

Half and Whole Notes

Let's take a look at notes and their relative values. You are already familiar with quarter notes, having played them in the previous exercises. As you know, a quarter note equals one beat. You also know that four quarter notes equal four beats. For example, in **Exercise 9** the time signature is 4/4, telling you that there are four quarter beats per measure. Measures 1, 3, 5, 7, and 9 have four quarter notes in each of those measures.

You are also familiar with the quarter rest, which equals a quarter beat of silence, and the half rest, which equals two beats of silence. A half note looks like a white quarter note and equals two beats of sound. The sound of a half note is sustained, or held, for two beats. For example, in **Exercise 10**, the first note is a half note and represents the first and second beats in the measure. This is followed by a quarter note for the third beat and another quarter note for the fourth beat. When playing a half note, you hold the sound through the second beat.

Whole notes look like half notes without stems. They are held for a full four beats. Whole rests look like upside-down half rests and receive four counts of silence. You can find a whole note in the first exercise in the next chapter (**Exercise 12**).

Adding the Fourth and Fifth Fingers

Now let's add fingers 4 and 5 to the exercises. Place your fifth finger above the G key (five keys above middle C), your fourth finger above the F key, your third finger above the E key, and your second finger above the D key.

Play **Exercise 10** starting with your fourth finger on the F key.

Exercise 10

Moderato

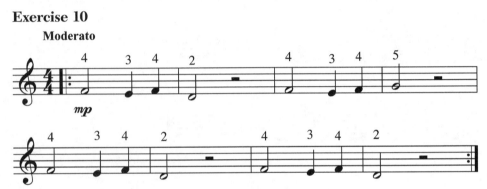

A new symbol has been added in **Exercise 10**: the dynamic marking *mp*. This symbol means *mezzo piano*, the Italian words for "medium soft."

Be sure to acknowledge the repeat sign in **Exercise 10**; at the end of measure 8, go directly back to the beginning of the piece (measure 1) and play the exercise again. Don't stop the even flow of beats when going from the end of measure 8 back to measure 1.

For the next exercise, place your fifth finger above the G key, your fourth finger above the F key, your third finger above the E key, your second finger above the D key, and your thumb above the C key (middle C). This exercise is designed to strengthen your fourth and fifth fingers, which are normally the weakest fingers in the right hand. (Reminder: Be sure to acknowledge the repeat sign.)

Play **Exercise 11** starting with your thumb on middle C. This is a good exercise to play frequently, as doing so will strengthen your fourth and fifth fingers.

Exercise 11

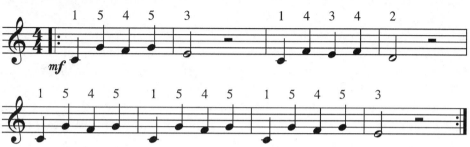

Practice, Practice, Practice

Now that you've played several exercises—and even your first tune—let's have a few words about practicing.

It's pretty basic: The more you practice, the better you sound. If you're really serious about learning how to play the piano, you should at a minimum practice ninety minutes a week in three thirty-minute practice sessions. And don't be restricted by your practice schedule. If you get the urge to play the piano, go ahead and play it. For the best use of your practice time, practice at the time of day or night that is free of any interruptions. Once you start your practice session, don't stop. It's very difficult to start and stop and try to start again.

 Piano Note

When playing all of these exercises, be sure to play the quarter notes evenly, giving them the same equal value (one beat). Be sure to also give the quarter and half rests their full values.

Learning how to play comes with time, desire, discipline, dedication, instruction, and a lot of practicing. Here are several things to keep in mind whenever you are playing the piano:

1. To avoid back pain, you have to sit at the piano with a straight spine. Do not lean forward or slouch. In the interest of comfort, sit on a cushion. If you purchase a used piano, be sure to get a matching piano bench and, if possible, a padded one. New pianos come with a matching piano bench, and some are padded.

2. Adjustable piano benches are preferred because you can adjust the height according to your size and finger placement on the keyboard. You want to be sitting high enough so your fingers and forearms are slightly higher than the keyboard, making it easy to press down on the keys. If you don't have an adjustable bench, then use cushions or pillows to get the height you need.

3. Don't put your fingers too far forward toward the back of the keys. Instead, place them closer to the edge, or the front, of the keys. This will give you a quicker and better response in pressing and releasing the piano keys.

Finding a Good Piano Teacher

This book is titled *The Only Basic Piano Instruction Book You'll Ever Need*. It is not, however the only piano *instruction* you'll ever need. Following the instructions in this book and doing its exercises as well as you can will get you headed down the road to becoming a proficient pianist. To truly arrive at that destination, though, you will need to find a good piano teacher to help you along the way.

There are a lot of piano teachers to choose from. Some teachers are faculty members at accredited music conservatories, colleges, or universities. Others teach at local music stores. Some teach in their homes where they have set up a home piano studio. You might prefer the formality of an academic setting, or you might be more comfortable in the more casual environment of the local music store or the teaching-from-home piano teacher.

In all cases, find out what the teachers' qualifications are and whether or not they are in good standing with professional music teachers' associations. Find out where they studied and what diplomas or degrees were earned. If you haven't already heard them play, ask them to play the piano for you.

But even the most qualified piano teacher might not be right for you. It depends on how much discipline you want from your teacher. Some teachers are more rigid than others. Some teachers are nicer than others. Once you know that a teacher has the necessary teaching skills, it really boils down to personality. You want to like and admire your teacher. Ask your prospective teachers a lot of questions, such as:

1. How long have you been teaching?
2. Why do you teach the piano?
3. How many students do you currently have?
4. What is your method of teaching?
5. How often should I practice?
6. What can I expect to accomplish after six months of lessons?
7. Why should I take piano lessons from you?

Teaching piano—as with teaching anything—requires the ability to effectively communicate with the student at each lesson. The best piano teachers are the ones who know how to motivate and encourage their students and give them the necessary constructive criticism. If you find that this is not the sort of relationship you have with your piano teacher, feel free to look for a new one.

Piano Note

After you've been playing the piano for a few months, record yourself playing your favorite piece of music. Listening to your playing is a very telling experience. When you're actually playing the piano, you're focused on playing the music to the best of your ability. When you listen to the playback of a recording, you'll hear things you didn't hear when you were playing. This allows you to critique yourself, hear any imperfections, and make adjustments in your playing.

three

Time to Add
Your Left Hand

BY THIS POINT, you've become pretty comfortable playing the piano with your right hand. Now, you'll start using your left hand to create foundations for the melodies your right hand will be playing. By the end of this chapter, you'll reach an important step, as you put both hands together to play a short piece of music.

Playing the Bass Line

For the most part, the left hand plays the bass line in a piece of music, which provides harmony to the melody played with the right hand. In more advanced piano compositions, the left hand plays both bass lines and chords, but for now let's concentrate on using the left hand to play just the bass line.

Fig. C: Abbreviated keyboard

5. 4. 3. 2. 1. - the fingers of your left hand

Let's assign numbers to the fingers of your left hand. Your thumb is 1, your index finger is 2, your middle finger is 3, your forefinger is 4, and your fifth finger is 5. Referring to **Fig. C**, place the five fingers of your left hand above the following keys: thumb above middle C, index finger above the B key, middle finger above the A key, forefinger above the G key, and fifth finger above the F key.

When playing with your left hand, the corresponding notes are written on a staff using the bass clef. As you can see in **Fig. D** below, the bass clef has two dots immediately to the right of the curved, half-heart-shaped half circle.

Fig. D: Bass clef

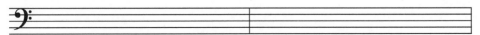

Starting with the top line and going down to the bottom line, the letter names of the lines of the bass staff are: A, F, D, B, and G. The letter names of the spaces from the top space to the bottom space are: G, E, C, and A. The F line is between the two dots of the bass clef.

Middle C plays a very important role in tying together the bass clef and the treble clef. As you can see in **Fig. E**, one ledger line above the bass clef is middle C, which is the same middle C located one ledger line below the treble clef.

Fig. E

In **Fig. E**, the time signature is 2/4. This time signature tells you two things: The top number tells you how many beats there are per measure (two) and the bottom number tells you the quarter note gets the beat.

As indicated in **Fig. E**, play the notes C, B, A, G, and F with the corresponding fingers of your left hand.

In the next exercise, **Exercise 12**, the fingering of the left hand starts on middle C in measure 1. In measure 3, the sequence begins with the thumb on B. In measure 5, the sequence begins with the thumb on A. And in measure 7, the sequence begins with the thumb on G.

The very last note in this exercise is C, which is one octave below middle C.

Exercise 12

Moderato

The first note in **Exercise 13** is C, located one octave below middle C. Place your fifth finger above the C key, fourth above the D key, third above the E key, second above the F key, and your thumb above the G key. Keeping your fingers in this position, play **Exercise 13**.

Exercise 13

A few new symbols have been added to **Exercise 13**. The word *allegro* indicates the tempo, which means "fast." The *f* dynamic marking, which represents *forte*, means "loud."

Start the exercise slowly. Once you have worked out the notes and rhythm, increase your speed and play the exercise loudly.

Fig. F: Abbreviated keyboard

* = the first note in exercise 14   ** = one octave below middle C

The term *octave* is a derivative of the Latin word *octava*, which means "eight." The low note C in **Exercise 13**, for example, is an octave below middle C.

The first note in **Exercise 14** is A, located two keys below the last note C in **Exercise 13** (please see **Fig. F**). Starting with your fifth finger on the A key, play **Exercise 14**.

Exercise 14

Adagio

There's a new tempo marking in **Exercise 14**, *adagio*, which means to play the exercise slowly. Did you acknowledge the repeat sign and play the exercise twice?

Playing Octaves with the Left Hand

In order to play an octave, you have to open up and stretch your left hand. The low note is played with your fifth finger, and the high note (located an octave above) is played with your thumb.

Place your fifth finger on the low C key and your thumb on middle C and play **Exercise 15**. This is a good exercise to play often, so you can get accustomed to stretching the fingers on your left hand and getting the feel of playing octaves.

Exercise 15

Playing Eighth Notes

In the next exercise, you're going to play eighth notes. Eighth notes are a subdivision of quarter notes. In other words, two eighth notes equal one quarter note. As you can see in measures 2, 4, 7, and 9 in **Exercise 16**, there are two eighth notes for the third and fourth beats of each measure. In measure 2, the third beat is comprised of the two eighth notes E and D, and the eighth notes C and B make up the fourth beat. Your goal is to play the eighth notes evenly within the third and fourth beats of the measure.

As you can see from the fingering in the following exercise, your thumb will be playing more than one key; it will play the A, G, F, and E keys. You will discover that the thumb on your left hand will be very active when playing bass lines.

Exercise 16

32

Exercise 16 continued

In **Exercise 17** you're going to play a series of eighth notes in every measure except the last measure, which has a whole note. With the steady flow of eighth notes, this exercise is designed to help you play the eighth notes evenly.

Start playing this exercise slowly. When you have worked out the placement of notes on the keyboard and the corresponding fingering, increase your speed to the designated allegro tempo.

Exercise 17

Allegro

Playing with Both Hands

By now, you should have a good feel for playing bass lines using the left hand. Are you ready to put both the left and right hands together?

Before you start playing a piano piece written for both hands, keep the following practice techniques in mind:

1. Start with only playing the right-hand part. Keep playing the right-hand part until you have perfected it and, if possible, have memorized it.
2. Once you have accomplished that, move on to the left hand. Now play only the left-hand part and keep playing it until you have perfected it.
3. Try your best to play either the right- or left-hand part automatically, without having to think about what you're playing; try to play the part instinctively. This will make it a lot easier when putting both hands together and playing both parts simultaneously.
4. Don't try to play the whole piece at once. Instead, take it one measure at a time. Once you have perfected measure 1, add the second measure. Before going on to the third measure, repeat measures 1 and 2 until they flow together without any hesitation or pauses. Keep adding measures, one at a time, until you have played them all.
5. Start playing it slowly. Once you are comfortable with the parts, increase the tempo.

Considering all of the above, play **Exercise 18**.

Exercise 18

Moderato

Let's take a closer look at **Exercise 18**. As you can see, this is the first exercise that uses two staffs—one for the right hand (treble clef) and one for the left hand (bass clef). A bracket ties the two staffs together.

In measures 1 and 2, the right hand plays whole notes while the left hand plays quarter notes. As you can plainly see, the whole note equals four quarter notes. Likewise, the four quarter notes equal the whole note. In the third measure, the half note E, played by the right hand, equals the two quarter notes C and B, played by the left hand. The same note values occur with the second half note F, played by the right hand, and the two quarter notes A and B, played by the left hand.

As indicated by the time signature, **Exercise 18** is in 4/4 time. The first beat in measure 1 has two notes: the whole note in the right hand and the quarter note in the left hand. Both of these notes are to be played at exactly the same time. In the first beat of the second measure, the F note in the right hand and the F note in the left hand are to be played at exactly the same time. Incidentally, the distance between the F note in the left hand and the F note in the right hand is an octave. In the first beat of the third measure, the E note in the right hand and middle C in the left hand are to be played at the same time. In the third beat of this same measure, the F note in the right hand and the A note in the left hand are to be played at the same time. Finally, in the first beat of the last measure, the exercise is concluded with the right hand playing the whole note E and the left hand playing the whole note middle C.

Piano Note

When playing the piano using both hands and reading the corresponding music, a vertical and horizontal sound experience occurs simultaneously. The vertical sound occurs when two notes are played at the same time. For instance in **Exercise 18**, measure 1, the right hand plays the E while the left hand plays the middle C below it. Looking at the written music, you see the vertical relationship of the E above the middle C. Once this vertical sound occurs, the horizontal sound takes place with the descending bass notes of the left hand. Your eyes are reading the music both vertically and horizontally at the same time.

Putting the Thumb Under the Fingers

There are eight white keys from middle C down to the C key an octave lower. When playing descending bass lines with your left hand that span an octave, you can run out of fingers. For instance, after playing the A with your third finger in **Exercise 19**, how do you play five more notes? By putting your thumb under your third finger. If F is your lowest note and middle C is your highest note, then you don't have to alter the fingering. However, if you have to play all eight notes from middle C down to the C located an octave lower, then your thumb is going to go under your middle finger.

Exercise 19

As the fingering indicates, after playing the third quarter note in the first measure with your third finger, the next note is to be played with the first finger of your left hand. The way to do this is to move your thumb under your third finger immediately after playing the A note. In doing so, you will be repositioning the fingers of your left hand to be able to play all of the notes down to the low C without running out of fingers.

Play **Exercise 19** slowly and keep repeating it until you are comfortable with this new fingering technique. In playing the repeat, you will be leaping an octave from the last note C (played with your fifth finger) up to the first note middle C (played with your thumb).

Leaping over the Thumb

When playing ascending bass notes with the left hand, you have to leap your finger over the thumb to avoid running out of fingers. As indicated in **Exercise 20**, in the third measure after playing the G note with your thumb, move your middle finger over your thumb to play the A note. The last two ascending notes are played with your second finger playing the B note and your thumb playing middle C.

Exercise 20 will help you to learn to play both descending and ascending bass notes, moving the thumb under your fingers on the way down and moving your middle finger over the thumb on the way up. Play this exercise slowly and keep repeating it until you get comfortable with the descending and ascending fingering.

Exercise 20

Putting It All Together

Exercise 21 is a piece of music that incorporates a lot of the material covered in this chapter. Before you play it, take a close look at all of the elements that make up the piece. Notice the rhythm of the right hand, which is comprised of a two-bar sequence made up of two eighth notes followed by two quarter notes, two more eighth notes, and a whole note in the second bar. The left hand plays a series of half notes, with fingering that includes the thumb going under the middle finger in measure 5. The tempo is moderate and the dynamic level is medium soft.

It's very important to look at all of the elements in a piece of music before you play it. This allows you to get mentally prepared and to anticipate what you have to do in order to perform it properly and play what's written.

Refresh your memory and look over the tips listed earlier in this chapter about practicing techniques to use when playing a piano piece with both hands.

When you are mentally prepared, play **Exercise 21** and enjoy this simple little tune.

LAZY DAY

four

Sharp Key
Signatures

CAUTION! MUSIC THEORY AHEAD! As you work your way through this chapter on key signatures, scale degrees, and the Circle of Fifths (something you may have thought, up to now, was a place in *The Lord of the Rings*), take your time. Be sure to read, re-read (and maybe re-re-read) each section until you understand it completely; and play the exercises until you can do them naturally. What you'll learn here is basic to everything that follows.

C Major

All of the exercises and piano pieces in this book so far have one thing in common: They are all in the key of C major or A minor. The key of C major and its relative minor, A minor, have no sharps or flats—you only play the white keys. The vast majority of sharps and flats are located on the black keys on the keyboard.

The key of A minor is C major's relative minor because it uses the same key signature, which has no sharps or flats. Notes that have no sharps or flats are also called naturals; they're natural—not sharp or flat. So all the notes in the C-major scale and the A-minor scale are natural.

Key signatures tell you what the notes are in a specific scale and what the corresponding keys are on the keyboard. Having played the exercises in the last chapter, you are already familiar with the key of C major. The consecutive sequence of eight notes from middle C up an octave to the C on the third space of the treble staff is called a scale. Let's take a look at the C-major scale.

Exercise 22

Moderato

As you can see, the notes in the C-major scale are C, D, E, F, G, A, B, and C. Scales go up, scales go down, and scales in a specific key are the same in all octaves.

The notes in scales are numbered from one to eight.

1. C is the root; also called the tonic.
2. D is the supertonic.
3. E is the mediant.
4. F is the subdominant.
5. G is the dominant.
6. A is the submediant.
7. B is the leading tone.
8. C is the octave.

All of these scale degrees have an intervallic relationship with the root C. An interval is the distance between any two pitches or notes. For instance, the intervallic distance between C and D is a second, between C and E is a third, between C and F is a fourth, and so forth.

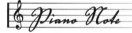

If the C-major scale sounds familiar to you, it may be because it is the same scale as the "do-re-mi-fa-so-la-ti-do" that you probably learned in elementary school, or perhaps remember from a song in *The Sound of Music*. Having no sharps or flats and using only white keys on the piano, the C-major scale is the simplest one to begin with during basic musical instruction.

Practice the C-major scale in **Exercise 22** with your right hand. Notice that the thumb goes under the middle finger on the third beat in measure 1, and the middle finger goes over the thumb on the fourth beat in measure 3. Repeat this exercise several times.

In the next exercise you're going to play the C-major scale with your left hand. Notice that the middle finger goes over the thumb on the first beat in measure 2 and that the thumb goes under the middle finger on the second beat in measure 3. Repeat **Exercise 23** several times.

Exercise 23

Moderato

In **Exercise 24** you're going to play the C-major scale covering two octaves, from middle C to the C two ledger lines above the treble staff. As indicated in the fingering, when you see 1 after 3 and 4, the thumb goes under the middle finger going up the scale. And going down the scale, when you see 3 and 4 after 1, the middle finger goes over the thumb.

Exercise 24

Moderato

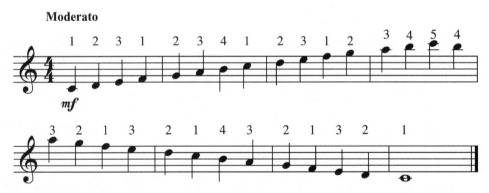

Moving on to the left hand, play the C scale covering two octaves in the bass in Exercise 25. Before you do, notice that in the fingering on the way up the scale, the middle finger goes over the thumb in measure 2, the fourth finger goes over the thumb in measure 3, and the middle finger goes over the thumb in measure 4. On the way down the scale, the thumb goes under the middle finger in measure 5 and under the fourth finger and third finger in measure 6. The first note is two octaves below middle C.

Exercise 25

Moderato

Next you are going to play the C-major scale at the distance of two octaves. Notice that **Exercise 26** is a combination of **Exercises 24 and 25**.

Exercise 26

Moderato

As you can see in the next exercise, the fingering for the left hand and the right hand is exactly the same as the fingering in **Exercise 26**. In **Exercise 27** play the A-minor scale at a distance of two octaves between both hands.

Exercise 27

Understanding the Circle of Fifths

Music theory is very logical. All of the notes in music are in alphabetical order from A to G. The treble and bass staffs are joined by the common note middle C. Notes from high ledger lines above the treble staff to ledger lines below the bass staff follow the musical alphabetical order.

In terms of the sequence of key signatures with sharps, they follow a circle of fifths. For example, the first sharp key signature, using one sharp, is the key of G, which happens to be five notes (a fifth) above C.

Table 1 is a visual representation of the Circle of Fifths. It is easy to see, for example, that the major key of E has a relative minor of C-sharp. Both keys contain four sharps.

Table 1

Major Key	Relative Minor Key	Number of Sharps and Flats	Sharps or Flats
C	A	none	all naturals
G	E	1 sharp	F
D	B	2 sharps	F, C
A	F-sharp	3 sharps	F, C, G
E	C-sharp	4 sharps	F, C, G, D
B	G-sharp	5 sharps	F, C, G, D, A
F-sharp	D-sharp	6 sharps	F, C, G, D, A, E
C-sharp	A-sharp	7 sharps	F, C, G, D, A, E, B
F	D	1 flat	B
B-flat	G	2 flats	B, E
E-flat	C	3 flats	B, E, A
A-flat	F	4 flats	B, E, A, D
D-flat	B-flat	5 flats	B, E, A, D, G
G-flat	E-flat	6 flats	B, E, A, D, G, C
C-flat	A-flat	7 flats	B, E, A, D, G, C, F

All major keys follow the same scale degrees and relationships of intervals. Using the C-major scale as an example, the distance between C and the seventh scale degree B is a half-step. Looking at your keyboard, you can see that the B key is right next to the C key. In the key of C, there are two half-steps: between B and C, and between E and F. The relationships among the other notes in the key of C are whole steps. For example, going from C to D is a whole step; there is a black key between the two notes. It's also a whole step from D to E, F to G, G to A, and A to B. As you can see on your keyboard, there are black keys between each of these whole steps.

All major key signatures have the very same whole-step/half-step pattern, which is:

- A whole step from the root to the second scale degree.

- A whole step from the second to third scale degree.
- A half-step from the third to fourth scale degree.
- A whole step from the fourth to fifth scale degree.
- A whole step from the fifth to sixth scale degree.
- A whole step from the sixth to seventh scale degree.
- A half-step from the seventh scale degree to the octave.

In summary, there are two half-steps and five whole steps in all major key signatures. The half-steps are from the third to fourth scale degrees and from the seventh scale degree to the octave.

G Major

Using this parallel whole-step/half-step relationship, the seventh scale degree in the key of G has to be a half-step away from the octave G. That's why the F is sharp. So when playing the G-major scale, you're going to play the black key between the F and G keys, which is called F-sharp. In **Exercise 28**, a sharp sign (♯) is on the F line in the treble clef, telling you to play the black key F-sharp. Be sure to play all of the F notes F-sharp, even though there isn't a sharp sign on the F space in the staff. With that in mind, play **Exercise 28** with your right hand.

Exercise 28

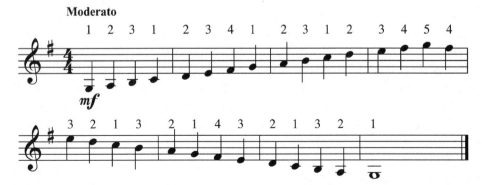

In keeping with the parallel logic of music theory, since C major's relative minor is A minor, G major's relative minor is E minor. The relative parallel connection is that the relative minors are built on the sixth scale degree of the major key. In the key of C major, the sixth scale degree is A, and in the key of G major, the sixth scale degree is E.

G is the root, the tonic.
A is the second, the supertonic.
B is the third, the mediant.
C is the fourth, the subdominant.

D is the fifth, the dominant.
E is the sixth, the submediant.
F is the seventh, the leading tone.
G is the eighth, the octave.

Both G major and E minor use the same key signature, which has one sharp—F-sharp. In the key of E minor, the scale degrees are:

E is the root, the tonic.
F-sharp is the second, the supertonic.
G is the third, the mediant.
A is the fourth, the subdominant.

B is the fifth, the dominant.
C is the sixth, the submediant.
D is the seventh, the subtonic.
E is the eighth, the octave.

It's important to note that all natural minor scales have a different whole-step/half-step pattern than major scales. In minor scales, the pattern is:

- A whole step from the root to the second scale degree.
- A half-step from the second to the third scale degree.
- A whole step from the third to the fourth scale degree.
- A whole step from the fourth to the fifth scale degree.
- A half-step from the fifth to the sixth scale degree.
- A whole step from the sixth to the seventh scale degree.
- A whole step from the seventh to the eighth scale degree.

In natural minor key signatures, the half-steps are from the second to third scale degree and from the fifth to sixth scale degree.

When playing **Exercise 29**, please note that the F-sharp is the second note in the E-minor scale and is played with the second finger on your right hand and the fourth finger on your left hand.

Exercise 29

Notice the 3/4 time signature in **Exercise 30**. That tells you there are three beats per measure and the quarter note gets the beat. This time signature creates a different feel from the customary 4/4 time signature. Time signatures that are in 2/4 and 4/4 create an even feel—the numbers are even—whereas a 3/4 is uneven because of the number three.

In **Exercise 30** you can see a series of three quarter notes per measure in the left hand, except for measures 16 and 24, which have dotted half notes. The series of three quarter notes will help you keep a steady 3/4 time. In order to get comfortable with the 3/4 time signature, look at the quarter notes and count *one, two, three*. The first beat of each measure is a little more pronounced than the second and third beats. The first beat is called the downbeat; the second and third beats are called upbeats. Downbeats are generally stronger than upbeats.

Look at the notes in the right hand in measures 1, 3, 4, 5, 7, 8, 9, 11, 12, 13, 14, 17, 19, 20, 21, and 24, and you'll see dotted half notes. The dot represents half the value of a half note, which is equal to one quarter note. Therefore, a dotted half note equals three quarter notes—the half note equals two quarter beats, and the dot equals one quarter beat. These three beats satisfy the 3/4 time signature, which tells you that there are three beats per measure.

In measures 3, 4, 7, 8, 11, 12, 13, 14, 19, and 20, the dotted half notes are tied to each other. This means you hold the dotted E in measure 3 through the end of measure 4. The collective value of the two dotted half notes tied together equals six beats, tying together the three beats in measure 3 with the three beats in measure 4. When you play the E in measure 3, keep that key depressed through the end of measure 4. In doing so, the sound will continue through both measures. The same is true in measures 7 and 8, 11 and 12, 13 and 14, and 19 and 20. Please observe the whole rests in the right hand in measures 15 and 16.

Piano Note

Music in major keys tends to be bright and cheerful. On the other hand, music in minor keys can sound introspective, moody, and even sad. **Exercise 30**, for example, is written in E minor, and it should create an introspective mood.

Exercise 30

LATE AT NIGHT

Exercise 30 continued

Also look at the fingering of both hands before playing the piece (the left-hand fingering is the same throughout). Notice the tempo marking *andante*, the metronome marking quarter note equals 108, and the dynamic marking *mp*. *Andante* means "moderately slow." If you have a metronome, set it to quarter note equals 108, and you will hear the rate of the pulse of the quarter note. The metronome marking makes the tempo marking much more specific.

In the left hand, the third note in measures 1, 5, 17, 21, and 23 is on two ledger lines above the bass staff, which is one octave above the first note in these measures. This ledger line is two whole steps above middle C. It is also the exact same pitch as the tied dotted half notes in measures 3 and 4, 7 and 8, and 19 and 20.

And because **Exercise 30** is in E minor, the key signature has an F-sharp in both the treble and bass clefs. In honoring the key signature, be sure to play the F-sharps. Even though there is only one sharp symbol on the top line of the treble clef and one sharp symbol on the second from the top line of the bass clef, all Fs have to be played sharp. The first and third notes played by the right hand in the second measure are F-sharps.

Once you have studied it and are mentally prepared, play this exercise starting with only the left-hand part. Then add the right hand, one measure at a time.

D Major

As we go through the circle of fifths, we'll be adding one sharp at a time for each new key signature.

The next key signature in the circle of fifths is D major, a fifth above G. The key of D major has two sharps: F-sharp (carried over from G major) and C-sharp. As with all major key signatures, there has to be a half-step from the seventh scale degree to the octave and a half-step from the third to the fourth scale degree. Therefore, the C is raised to a C-sharp, and the F is raised to an F-sharp.

If the relative minor of C major is A minor, and the relative minor of G major is E minor, what is the relative minor of D major? Knowing the relative minor is built on the sixth scale degree of every major scale, B minor is D major's relative minor. B minor and D major use the same key signature, which has two sharps: F-sharp and C-sharp.

In the next exercise, you're going to see a different fingering pattern for the left hand when playing the B-minor scale. As indicated, you start with your fourth finger instead of the customary fifth finger when playing C- and G-major scales and A- and E-minor scales. Be sure to catch the over-the-thumb action going up the scale and the under-the-thumb action on the way down.

With that in mind, play **Exercise 31** with the left hand, starting with the low B, located below the second ledger line below the bass clef.

Exercise 31

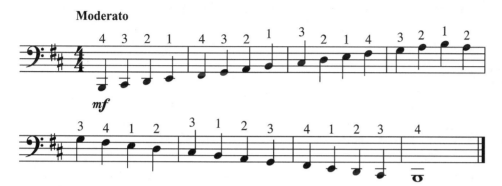

Move on to **Exercise 32** and put your hands together to play the B-minor scale up and down two octaves. Be sure to catch the under-the-thumb action in the right hand going up the scale and the over-the-thumb action going down the scale.

Exercise 32

In **Exercise 33**, play the D-major scale with both hands.

Exercise 33

Now that you are familiar with the D-major and B-minor scales, let's take a close look at the next exercise. This piece is designed to strengthen all of the fingers in your right hand. It is composed utilizing a sequence of a quarter note followed by six eighth notes. As the metronome marking indicates (quarter note equals 92), **Exercise 34** is slower than **Exercise 30**. Given its title, the piece is to be played lightly and, as the dynamic marking indicates, medium soft.

Make your preparations and enjoy this light little piece.

Exercise 34

QUITE LIGHTLY

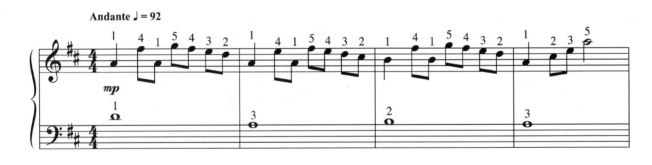

A Major

So far we have covered C major (A minor), G major (E minor), and D major (B minor). A fifth above D is A. Therefore, the next key in the circle of fifths is A major and its relative minor, F-sharp minor.

There are three sharps in the key of A major and F-sharp minor: F-sharp, C-sharp, and G-sharp. In the next exercise, you will be playing the A-major scale with both hands. Start playing with only the right hand, then move on to only the left hand, and eventually put both hands together.

Exercise 35

In the next exercise, please notice the different fingering for both hands when playing the F-sharp minor scale.

E Major

The next sharp key is E major and its relative minor, C-sharp minor. E major and C-sharp minor have four sharps in the key signature: F-sharp, C-sharp, G-sharp, and D-sharp. Play **Exercise 37** starting with the right hand and eventually add the left hand.

Exercise 37

In **Exercise 38**, please notice the different fingering in both hands when playing the C-sharp–minor scale. Similar to F-sharp minor, the fingering is different because the scale starts on a black key.

Exercise 38

B Major

Continuing on with the circle of fifths, the next sharp key is B major and its relative minor, G-sharp minor. The new sharp added to this key signature is A-sharp, the seventh scale degree in B major. The five sharps in B major and G-sharp minor are: F-sharp, C-sharp, G-sharp, D-sharp, and A-sharp.

By now you have probably noticed the pattern in the addition of sharps: The new sharp is always a fifth above the previous sharp. For example, in the key of E major, the fourth sharp is D. B major uses the same four sharps in E major plus the new sharp A. A-sharp is a fifth above D-sharp.

Before playing the B-major scale, notice that the fingering in the left hand starts with the fourth finger. And watch out for those A-sharps!

Exercise 39

The fingering for playing the G-sharp–minor scale is the same as the fingering for the C-sharp–minor scale—the right hand starts with the second finger, and the left hand starts with the third finger. Here's the G-sharp–minor scale in action.

Exercise 40

F-Sharp Major

In the next key signature, you're going to discover a sharp that isn't on a black key. In the F-sharp–major scale, the seventh scale degree (which you know has to be raised a half-step) is E-sharp. As you also know, E-natural is the white key on the piano, two whole steps above C. When raising E a half-step and making it E-sharp, it happens to be the same pitch as F, which is one white key above E.

With that in mind, play the F-sharp–major scale in **Exercise 41**.

Exercise 41

Here's the D-sharp–minor scale, which uses the same key signature as F-sharp major. Notice the different fingering in both hands and watch out for those E-sharps!

Exercise 42

Let's review the key signatures. The sequence of key signatures in the circle of fifths starting with C major (and their relative minors) is:

Major Key Signature	Relative Minor
C major	A minor
G major	E minor
D major	B minor
A major	F-sharp minor
E major	C-sharp minor
B major	G-sharp minor
F-sharp major	D-sharp minor

As you can see, the relative minors also follow the circle of fifths: E minor is a fifth above A minor; B minor is a fifth above E minor, and so forth.

The major sharp key signatures and their relative minors have:

No sharps—C major, A minor
One sharp (F-sharp)—G major, E minor
Two sharps (F-sharp, C-sharp)—D major, B minor
Three sharps (F-sharp, C-sharp, G-sharp)—A major, F-sharp minor
Four sharps (F-sharp, C-sharp, G-sharp, D-sharp)—E major, C-sharp minor
Five sharps (F-sharp, C-sharp, G-sharp, D-sharp, A-sharp)—B major, G-sharp minor
Six sharps (F-sharp, C-sharp, G-sharp, D-sharp, A-sharp, E-sharp)—F-sharp major, D-sharp minor

Continuing the Circle of Fifths

We have covered the most common sharp key signatures used in piano music, and music in general. However, sharp key signatures do continue beyond F-sharp major. Continuing on with the circle of fifths, the remaining major sharp key signatures and their relative minors are:

C-sharp major, A-sharp minor
G-sharp major, E-sharp minor
D-sharp major, B-sharp minor

Even though you probably won't play piano pieces written in these key signatures, you should be aware of them.

five

**Flat Key
Signatures**

NOW THAT YOU HAVE LEARNED the sharp key signatures thoroughly, learning the flat key signatures (and, yes, the Circle of Fourths) should not be so difficult. And more good news: At the end of this chapter, you'll have covered all the key signatures you need to know—music just has sharp and flat ones, no "dull" or "round" ones—and you'll be able to move on to chords.

Understanding the Circle of Fourths

Sharp key signatures follow a circle of fifths. Sharps raise any given pitch up a half-step. Flats, on the other hand, lower a pitch down a half-step. Flat key signatures follow a circle of fourths. Refer to the chart below to visualize this system.

The first flat key is F major. Going up four notes is B; however, in keeping with the whole-step/half-step scale degree pattern of major scales, the B is flat in F major. There has to be a half-step between the third and fourth scale degrees. F to G and G to A are whole steps; A to B-flat is a half-step. The B-flat is the black key located between A and B on your keyboard. In keeping with the whole-step/half-step pattern of minor key scales, there has to be a half-step from the fifth scale degree to the sixth scale degree. So in the key of D minor (which is F major's relative minor), the fifth scale degree is A, and a half-step above that is the sixth scale degree, B-flat.

As you recall, sharps are located on the seventh scale degree in major key signatures and on the second scale degree in their relative minor key signatures. For example, in the key of G major, the seventh scale degree is F-sharp; in E minor, F-sharp is the second scale degree. Unlike sharps, flats are located on the fourth scale degree in major key signatures and on the sixth scale degree in minor key signatures.

The major flat key signatures and their relative minors are:

Major Flat Key Signature	Relative Minor
F major	D minor
B-flat major	G minor
E-flat major	C minor
A-flat major	F minor
D-flat major	B-flat minor
G-flat major	E-flat minor

F Major

Play **Exercise 43** and take special note of the B-flat.

Exercise 43

By now, you're quite familiar with the way major scales sound. You're accustomed to scale degrees and the pattern of whole steps and half-steps. With that in mind, try a little experiment and play the F-major scale with B-natural (the white key), not B-flat (the black key). Your ears should tell you that the B-natural doesn't sound right because it's not in the key signature.

In the next exercise, play the D-minor scale, which uses the same key signature as F major.

Exercise 44

B-Flat Major

Moving up a fourth is the key signature of B-flat major and its relative minor, G minor. Notice that the fingering in the right hand starts with the second finger. The fingering in the left hand starts with the third finger.

As always, start playing **Exercise 45** with only the right hand. Then play with only the left hand. When you have both parts worked out, play the B-flat–major scale with both hands.

Exercise 45

Exercise 46 is a piano piece called "Octavia." (When you look at the left-hand part, you'll know why.) The key signature, which has the two flats B-flat and E-flat, tells you the piece is in the key of B-flat major. The time signature tells you the piece is in 4/4 time. The tempo is moderato, with a metronome marking of quarter note equals 108. The dynamic marking *mp* tells you to play the music medium soft. But then there's a new sign, which looks like a stretched-out part of a triangle. This is a crescendo sign, which means to play the music gradually louder by increasing the volume of sound. This pertains to the first four eighth notes: D, E-flat, F, and G. In the next measure, the *mf* dynamic marking tells you to play medium loud. So there is a gradual increase from medium soft to medium loud from the first eighth note D in measure 1 to the quarter note A in measure 2.

Unlike the other pieces you have played so far, **Exercise 46** starts off with rests—a whole rest in the left hand and a half rest in the right hand. What you have to do is count off and feel the first two beats, which are silent, and then play the eighth notes representing the third and fourth beats for the right hand. The four eighth notes in the first measure are called pick-up notes, which lead the way up to the downbeat (quarter note A) in measure 2.

Compositionally, **Exercise 46** uses a two-bar sequence, or motif, which is comprised of a half rest followed by four eighth notes followed by a quarter note, two eighth notes, and a half note. This two-bar sequence is repeated throughout the piece until measure 13, when the sequence is broken with two quarter notes (instead of four eighth notes) followed by a tied whole note.

Another dynamic sign appears in measure 15 that is just the opposite of the crescendo sign in measure 1. This is a decrescendo sign, which tells you to play the music softer. Because the right hand is holding the sound of the tied whole note, the decrescendo sign applies to the notes played in the left hand. In terms of volume, this piece starts off medium soft, gets medium loud, and ends medium soft.

Notice the fingering in the right hand in measures 9, 11, and 12. The thumb goes under the second finger to play the middle C in measures 9 and 11; and, in measure 12, the second finger goes over the thumb to play the half note B-flat.

Starting slowly with the right hand only, play **Exercise 46**.

Exercise 46

OCTAVIA

Exercise 46 continued

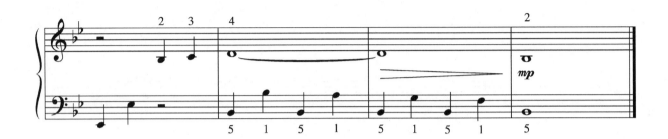

In **Exercise 47**, which is in the key of G minor, take a close look at the fingering in the right hand before playing it. As you will discover in the first measure, it feels natural to simply move the fifth finger of the right hand down a half-step from B-flat to A. In the third measure, the first note is played by the second finger by going over the thumb on the last note played in the preceding measure. In the third measure, the fifth finger moves down a half-step from E-flat to D. When playing this exercise, please observe the repeat sign.

Piano Note

A tip: If your piano bench is not padded, and you're not going to be playing for an extended period, putting a cushion or pillow on the bench will make a big difference as far as comfort.

The Only Basic Piano Instruction Book You'll Ever Need

Exercise 47

E-Flat Major

The next flat key signature in the circle of fourths is E-flat major and its relative minor, C minor. As you can see, E-flat major and C minor have three flats: B-flat, E-flat, and A-flat. In comparison with the evolution of sharp key signatures and their corresponding sharps, the addition of flats in flat key signatures follows the evolving circle of fourths. In other words, the first flat key signature, F major, has one flat: B-flat. The second flat key signature, B-flat major, has two flats: B-flat and E-flat. And the third flat key signature, E-flat major, has three flats.

In the next exercise, notice that the fingering in the right hand starts with the second finger, and the fingering in the left hand starts with the third finger. When going up the E-flat major scale, the thumb in the right hand will go under the fingers twice per each octave, and the third and fourth fingers go over the thumb on the way down. The fingering in the left hand starts with the third finger. On the way up the scale, the fourth and third fingers go over the thumb twice per each octave. On the way down the scale, the thumb goes under the fingers twice per octave.

With that in mind, play the E-flat–major scale in **Exercise 48** starting with the right hand.

Exercise 48

In **Exercise 49**, try your hand at E-flat's relative minor, C minor. And be sure to play the B-, E-, and A-flats!

Exercise 49

 Piano Note

The biggest difference in sound is between major and minor keys. But each major key has its own distinct sound. For instance, play the C-major scale. Then play the B-flat–major scale. Even though they're both major scales, they sound very different, largely because of the two flats in the B-flat scale: the B-flat and the E-flat. You may discover that C major sounds brighter than B-flat major. With minor scales, the difference in sound can be even more striking. For example, play the A-minor scale. Then play the C-minor scale. Here again, the difference is because of the three flats in the key of C minor. In the key of A minor, the B, E, and A are natural, and in C minor, the B, E, and A are flat.

In **Exercise 50**, the key signature tells you the song is in C minor. The time signature is in 4/4 time. The tempo is andante with a metronome marking of quarter note equals 96, and *mf* tells you to play the song medium loud.

In the first measure, the first three beats are silent (as indicated by the half rest and quarter rest), and the fourth beat has two eighth notes (E-flat and F), which are pick-ups leading up to the first quarter note in the second measure. In the sixth measure, notice that the last eighth note (E-flat) is played with the first finger as it goes over the thumb.

For those of you who are vocally inclined, you might want to sing along with the melody played by the right hand.

Exercise 50

DON'T YOU EVER LET ME DOWN

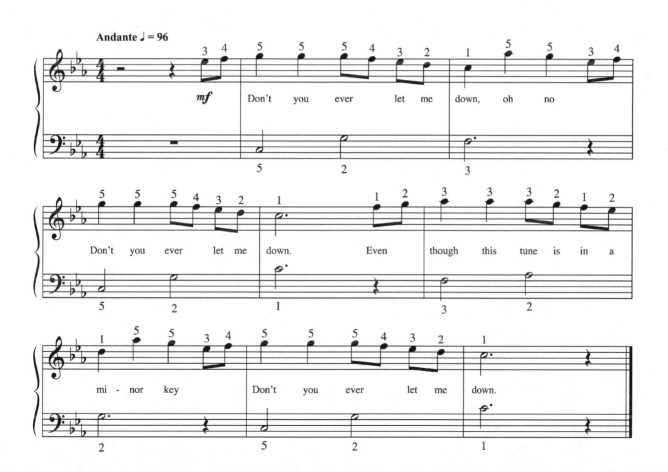

A-Flat Major

The next flat key is A-flat major and its relative minor, F minor. The new flat in this key is D-flat, which is the fourth scale degree in A-flat major and the sixth scale degree in F minor. As you can see in the fingering of both the right and left hands, a lot of under- and over-the-thumb action takes place while playing the A-flat–major scale in two octaves.

With that in mind, please play the A-flat–major scale, as shown in **Exercise 51**, starting with your second finger in the right hand and your third finger in the left hand.

Exercise 51

You'll notice the fingering in **Exercise 52** is quite different from the fingering of the A-flat–major scale in **Exercise 51**. With that in mind, play the F-minor scale in **Exercise 52**.

Exercise 52

Exercise 53, titled "Leaping Down a Fifth," is a challenging piece that is intended to get your right hand accustomed to moving from E-flat down a fifth to A-flat. In order to accomplish this, your third finger goes over the thumb, and your thumb goes under your third finger and leaps down to A-flat. As indicated in the fingering of the right hand in measures 8 and 16, the last eighth note is played with your third finger, while your thumb quickly goes under your fingers and plays the A-flat.

Exercise 53

LEAPING DOWN A FIFTH

Exercise 53 continued

The tempo of **Exercise 53** is allegro with a metronome marking of quarter note equals 126. Start playing the exercise slowly and gradually speed up to the allegro tempo. But before you do, be sure to note that the piece is written in the key of A-flat, which has four flats. So be sure to play Bs, Es, As, and Ds flat.

You should play only the right hand for the entire piece several times before adding the left hand. Be careful with the last four eighth notes in measure 20; they're one note higher than the sequence of eighth notes in measures 4 and 12. The fingering for the left hand is the same throughout the piece, alternating between the fifth finger and the thumb.

As you play the descending eighth notes in measures 8 and 16 and the following quarter note in measures 9 and 17, you might be able to hear why it's called "Leaping Down a Fifth."

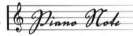

You may notice that in **Exercise 53**, "Leaping Down a Fifth," the piece starts off with the right hand, while the left hand rests for the first eight measures. One advantage of studying the piece before you play it is that you can then be sure to have the left hand ready in position from the beginning, resting lightly above A-flat and E-flat for the left hand in measure 9.

D-Flat Major

A fourth above A-flat gives us the next key signature, D-flat major, and its relative minor, B-flat minor. D-flat major has five flats: B-flat, E-flat, A-flat, D-flat, and the new flat, G-flat. With five flats in the key signature, you'll be playing five black keys and only two white keys on the keyboard. As a result, the fingering in the right hand starts with the second finger, and the fingering in the left hand starts with the third finger. At the top of the two-octave scale, the thumb on the right hand goes under the fingers to play the C, and the second finger goes over the thumb to play the high D-flat. Similarly, the thumb on the left hand plays the high C, and the second finger goes over the thumb to play the high D.

Exercise 54

Moderato

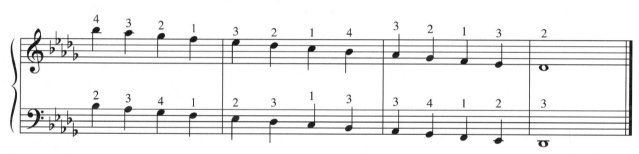

Exercise 55 is the B-flat–minor scale, which starts with the second finger on both hands.

Exercise 55

Enharmonic Equivalents

What's an enharmonic equivalent? An example: the pitch G-flat, which is located on the black key (one half-step lower than the white key G), is the same pitch as F-sharp (a half-step higher than F). G-flat and F-sharp are enharmonic equivalents; they are the same pitch—the same black key—but have different letter names.

In addition to individual notes having enharmonic equivalents, there are enharmonic equivalent scales. For example, when you play the D-flat–major scale, you're also playing the C-sharp–major scale. The pitches, the keys, and even the fingering are the same, but all of the letter names are different.

Looking at the letter names in both keys we have:

D-flat major	equals	C-sharp major
D-flat	=	C-sharp
E-flat	=	D-sharp
F	=	E-sharp
G-flat	=	F-sharp
A-flat	=	G-sharp
B-flat	=	A-sharp
C	=	B-sharp

So every note in the C-sharp–major scale is an enharmonic equivalent of the notes in the D-flat–major scale. Furthermore, the entire C-sharp–major scale is the enharmonic equivalent of the D-flat–major scale. Instead of having to play seven sharps in C sharp-major, simply play five flats in D-flat major.

The same is true with the relative minors. When you're playing the B-flat–minor scale, you're also playing the A-sharp–minor scale because B-flat and A-sharp are enharmonic equivalents.

G-Flat Major

Just as D-flat major is the enharmonic equivalent to C-sharp major, G-flat major is the enharmonic equivalent to F-sharp major. More than likely, if someone is going to write a piece of music in G-flat major, it will be written in the enharmonic equivalent key, F-sharp major.

Here are the note-for-note enharmonic equivalents in both keys:

G-flat major	equals	F-sharp major
G-flat	=	F-sharp
A-flat	=	G-sharp
B-flat	=	A-sharp
C-flat	=	B
D-flat	=	C-sharp
E-flat	=	D-sharp
F	=	E-sharp

So go back to Chapter 4 and play the F-sharp–major scale in **Exercise 41**. When playing the F-sharp–major scale, say the enharmonic equivalent letter names in G-flat major (G-flat, A-flat, B-flat, C-flat, D-flat, E-flat, and F). For all intents and purposes, you will have played the G-flat–major scale.

Here are the note-for-note enharmonic equivalents in both relative minor keys:

E-flat minor	equals	D-sharp minor
E-flat	=	D-sharp
F	=	E-sharp
G-flat	=	F-sharp
A-flat	=	G-sharp
B-flat	=	A-sharp
C-flat	=	B
D-flat	=	C-sharp

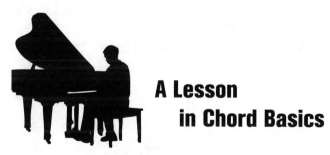

six

A Lesson
in Chord Basics

IN MUSICAL TERMS, harmony is the study of the structure, progression, and relation of chords. What's fascinating about music is the many different ways of arranging harmony juxtaposed to melody. For instance, with piano music, the right hand can play a simple melody, while the left hand can play consonant, harmonically pleasing chords or dissonant, unresolved chords. In this chapter, we'll focus on how chords can be used to create harmony, or as one dictionary definition has it, "a combination of sounds considered pleasing to the ear."

Major Chords

As mentioned, an interval is the measured distance between any two pitches. (For instance, in the key of D major, from the root D up to B is an interval of a sixth.) Chords are comprised of intervals. A D-major chord is the combination of two intervals: a major third from the root (D) up to the third scale degree (F-sharp), and a minor third from F-sharp up to the fifth scale degree (A). A major third contains two whole steps: D to E and E to F-sharp. A minor third contains one half-step, F-sharp to G, and one whole step, G to A. So a D-major chord contains the three notes D, F-sharp, and A. Three-note chords are also called triads.

All major chords follow the same two-interval formula: a major third followed by a minor third. Choose any pitch and make it the root of a major chord: Count up two whole steps and you have the third of the chord; count up a half-step and whole step above the third and you have the fifth. For example, with A-flat as the root, the third is C, and the fifth is E-flat.

Table 2 shows the construction of major triads (chords) starting with various roots:

Table 2

Root	Third	Fifth
C	E	G
C-sharp	E-sharp	G-sharp
D	F-sharp	A
E-flat	G	B-flat
E	G-sharp	B
F-sharp*	A-sharp*	C-sharp*

G-flat*	B-flat*	D-flat*
A	C-sharp	E
B	D-sharp	F-sharp

* enharmonic equivalents

Now let's apply these major chords to the keyboard. Starting with C major and using your right hand, place your thumb on middle C, your second finger on E, and your fifth finger on G. Strike the keys all at the same time. This right-hand finger configuration is the same for all major chords, and the same in any octave. For example, when you play the C-major chord an octave higher, use the same fingering. Please see **Fig. G**.

Fig. G: Root position major chords

Do the same with the rest of the major chords listed in the table (C-sharp, D, E-flat, E, F-sharp, G-flat, A, and B major chords). Be sure to acknowledge the specified sharps and flats per each chord. Also, when playing the C-sharp–major chord, notice the white key E-sharp. Look at **Fig. H** below.

Fig. H: Root position major chords

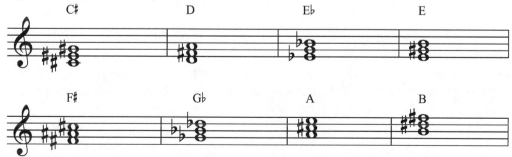

Minor Chords

The intervallic structure of all minor chords is comprised of two intervals: a minor third followed by a major third. For example, the D-minor chord has a minor third from the root, D, up to the third, F. This minor third interval is comprised of a whole step from D to E and a half-step from E to F. The D-minor chord has a major third from the third of the chord, F, up to the fifth, A. This major third interval is comprised of two whole steps, from F to G and G to A.

Here's a table showing the construction of minor triads (chords) starting with various roots.

Table 3

Root	Third	Fifth
C	E-flat	G
C-sharp	E	G-sharp
D	F	A
E-flat	G-flat	B-flat
E	G	B
F	A-flat	C
F-sharp	A	C-sharp
G	B-flat	D
A	C	E
B-flat	D-flat	F

Please note that all of the above minor chords have the same intervallic structure: a minor third followed by a major third.

The right-hand fingering of these minor chords is the same as the fingering used when playing major chords: thumb on the root, second finger on the third, and fifth finger on the fifth. With that in mind, please play the chords as shown in **Fig. I**.

92

Fig. I: Root position major chords

Minor Chords - Root Position

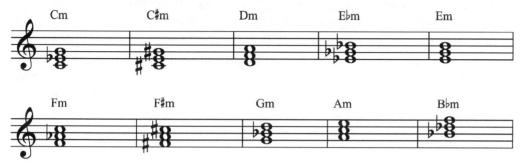

Playing Chords in a Major Key

When you played the C-major scale, you played the scale degrees from the root C up one or two octaves. A piece of music written in the key of C major can use all or some of the chords within the key. Chords in the key of C major are built on each scale degree.

Table 4 shows the chords in the key of C major and their intervallic structures and chord qualities.

Table 4

Scale Degree	Chord Number	Root	Third	Fifth	Quality
1st	I	C	E	G	major
2nd	ii	D	F	A	minor
3rd	iii	E	G	B	minor
4th	IV	F	A	C	major
5th	V	G	B	D	major
6th	vi	A	C	E	minor
7th	vii	B	D	F	diminished

Notice that each chord has a number and that all of the chords have their own root, third, and fifth. The major chords in the key of C are the I, IV, and V chords. They are major because they are comprised of two intervals: a major third and a minor third. For instance, the IV chord F has a major third from the root F to A and a minor third from A to C. Remember—the interval of a major third is comprised of two whole steps, and the interval of a minor third is comprised of one whole step and a half-step.

The minor chords in the key of C are the ii, iii, and vi chords. To make it easier to differentiate between the major and minor chords in a given key, the major chord numbers are in uppercase roman numerals, and the minor chords are in lowercase roman numerals. The D-, E-, and A-minor chords are minor because they are comprised of a minor third and a major third. Using the ii chord D minor for example, it's a whole step from D to E and a half-step from E to F (which makes up the interval of a minor third) and from F to G and G to A are two whole steps (which makes up the interval of a major third).

Diminished Chords

Chords built on the seventh scale degree are called diminished chords, which are a half-step smaller than minor chords. The intervallic structure of all diminished chords is comprised of two minor intervals. For instance, the B-diminished chord has a minor second from B to D (a half-step from B to C and a whole step from C to D) and another minor second from D to F-natural (a whole step from D to E and a half-step from E to F).

The chords in the key of C major are:

C major
D minor
E minor
F major
G major
A minor
B diminished

Exercise 56 utilizes some of the chords in the key of C played by the right hand.

There are twelve chords in this exercise. The rhythmic pattern is the same throughout—two quarter note chords followed by a half note chord per measure. As you can see, the chords are comprised of three-note triads, and the notes are stacked up together, making the chord. The sequence of chords is called a chord progression.

Please look at the table on p. 93 of the chords in C major carefully before playing **Exercise 56**.

Augmented Chords

Augmented notes are raised a half-step above the standard position in chords or scales. An augmented chord contains a root, a major third, and an augmented fifth. It's almost an ordinary major chord, but the fifth is one half-step higher.

Try playing a C-major chord: C, E, and G. Now raise the G a half step to G-sharp. C, E, and G-sharp is an augmented chord.

Table 5

Chord	Notes in the Chord	Chord Quality	Fingering
1st	C–E–G	I (major)	thumb-C, 2nd-E, 5th-G
2nd	B–D–G*	V (major)	thumb-B, 2nd-D, 5th-G
3rd	A–C–E	vi (minor)	thumb-A, 2nd-C, 5th-E
4th	A–C–E	vi (minor)	thumb-A, 2nd-C, 5th-E
5th	B–D–F	vii (diminished)	thumb-B, 2nd-D, 5th-F
6th	C–E–G	I (major)	thumb-C, 2nd-E, 5th-G
7th	C–F–A**	IV (major)	thumb-C, 2nd-F, 5th-A
8th	D–G–B**	V (major)	thumb-D, 2nd-G, 5th-B
9th	E–A–C**	vi (minor)	thumb-E, 2nd-A, 5th-C
10th	E–A–C**	vi (minor)	thumb-E, 2nd-A, 5th-C
11th	D–G–B**	V (major)	thumb-D, 2nd-G, 5th-B
12th	E–G–C*	I (major)	thumb-E, 2nd-G, 5th

* first inversion   ** second inversion

As the fingering indicates above, the right hand uses the same finger configuration for all of the chords in this exercise (thumb, second finger, and fifth finger).

Exercise 56

Let's add a left-hand bass line to the same chord progression for **Exercise 57**.

Exercise 57

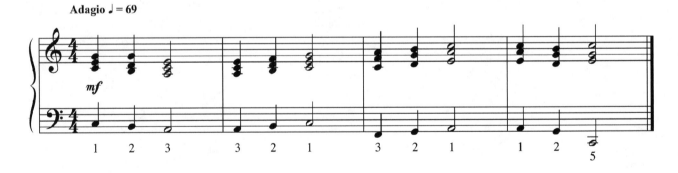

Root Position and First- and Second-Inversion Chords

The first, third, fourth, fifth, and sixth chords in **Exercise 57** are in root position, meaning that the first note in each chord is the root of the chord, followed by the third and fifth. However, the second chord and the chords in measures 3 and 4 are not in root position. The second chord in the first measure is in a first-inversion position, meaning that the first note in the chord is not the root, but the third, followed by the fifth and the root. Indicated with one asterisk in **Table 5** (in the section on augmented chords), the first note in the G-major chord is B, the third, followed by the fifth, D, and the root, G.

Chords seven through eleven are in a position called second inversion, meaning that the first note of the chord is the fifth, followed by the root and the third. Looking at **Table 5**, the second-inversion chords have two asterisks by their letter names. For example, in measure 3, the first note in the F-major chord is C, which is the fifth of the chord. Similar to the second chord in the first measure, the last chord in the exercise is also in a first-inversion position (the first note of the chord is the third, followed by the fifth and the root).

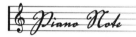

Listening to music is an acquired skill. It requires full attention, being focused, and not being distracted. With repeated listening to the same piece of music, you will hear things you didn't hear the first or second time. When you're playing a piece of music, give it your full listening attention. Listen to the melody; listen to the harmony and bass line. Listen to the parts individually, and listen to them collectively. Good musicians are very good listeners.

Chords in a Minor Key

When you played minor scales in Chapters 4 and 5, you played natural minor scales—notes that observe the key signature. For example, when you played the E-minor scale, you acknowledged the F-sharp key signature and played the series of notes E, F-sharp, G, A, B, C, D, and the octave E. That's the E-natural–minor scale.

When building chords on the scale degrees of E-natural minor we get the following chords:

Table 6

Scale Degree	Number	Root	Third	Fifth	Quality
1st	i	E	G	B	minor
2nd	ii	F-sharp	A	C	diminished
3rd	III	G	B	D	major
4th	iv	A	C	E	minor
5th	v	B	D	F-sharp	minor
6th	VI	C	E	G	major
7th	VII	D	F-sharp	A	major

As you can see by doing a comparison with the chords built on major scale degrees, the quality of chords are different in a natural minor key.

Chords built on major scale degrees have the following qualities:

- Major chords: I, IV, V
- Minor chords: ii, iii, vi
- Diminished chords: vii

Chords built on natural minor scale degrees have the following qualities:

- Major chords: III, VI, VII
- Minor chords: i, iv, v
- Diminished chords: ii

Harmonic minor scales are different from natural harmonic scales because of one scale degree: The seventh scale degree is sharp in a harmonic minor scale. As discussed earlier, the seventh scale degree in a natural minor scale is not sharp, it's natural. Using E minor as an example, the seventh scale degree is D-natural in E-natural minor, and D-sharp in E-harmonic minor. When applying the sharp seventh scale degree to chords in E-harmonic minor, the III chord (G) becomes augmented, the V chord (B) becomes major, and the vii chord (D) becomes diminished because of the D-sharp.

When building chords on the scale degrees of E-harmonic minor, we get the following chords:

Table 7

Scale Degree	Chord Number	Root	Third	Fifth	Quality
1st	i	E	G	B	minor
2nd	ii	F-sharp	A	C	diminished
3rd	III	G	B	D-sharp	augmented
4th	iv	A	C	E	minor
5th	V	B	D-sharp	F-sharp	major
6th	VI	C	E	G	major
7th	vii	D-sharp	F-sharp	A	diminished

Here's a comparison of chord qualities between natural minor scale degrees and harmonic minor scale degrees:

	Natural Minor	Harmonic Minor
Major chords	III, VI, VII	V, VI
Minor chords	i, iv, v	i, iv
Diminished chords	ii	ii, vii
Augmented chords		III

The most striking difference between these two different minor scales is the quality of the fifth scale degree. As mentioned earlier, the fifth scale degree is called the dominant. The dominant/tonic relationship is harmonically very strong because the dominant chord, built on the fifth scale degree, wants to resolve to the tonic, the root. This is referred to as tension/resolution in harmonic terms. Using E-harmonic minor as an example, the tension is caused by the D-sharp, which is the third in the V chord B major. Harmonically, the D-sharp wants to resolve to the tonic E. In the E-natural–minor scale, the fifth scale degree is B minor, with D-natural as the third in the B minor chord. The harmonic tension is less between B minor and E minor because of the D-natural.

The next two exercises illustrate these harmonic differences.

In **Exercise 58**, you will be playing chords in E-natural minor, acknowledging the D-natural in the root position VII chord (first half note chord in the second measure) and the root position v chord (first half note chord in the fourth measure). Likewise, the left hand plays a D-natural (second quarter note in the fourth measure).

Before playing the exercise take a close look at the following table.

Table 8

Chord	Notes in the Chord	Chord Position/Quality	Fingering
1st	E–G–B	i-minor/root	thumb-E, 2nd-G, 5th-B
2nd	E–A–C**	iv-minor/2nd	thumb-E, 2nd-A, 5th-C
3rd	D–F#–A	VII-major/root	thumb-D, 2nd-F#, 5th-A
4th	E–G–B	i-minor/root	thumb-E, 2nd-G, 5th-B
5th	B–E–G**	i-minor/2nd	thumb-B, 2nd-E, 5th-G
6th	A–C–E	iv-minor/root	thumb-A, 2nd-C, 5th-E
7th	B–D–F#	v-minor/root	thumb-B, 2nd-D, 4th-F#
8th	B–E–G**	i-minor/2nd	thumb-B, 2nd-E, 5th-G

** second-inversion chords

Exercise 58 has a repeat sign. Play this exercise the first time with only the right hand. If you need to, keep repeating only the right-hand part. Once you have the right-hand part worked out, play only the left-hand part. Then play the piece as written: once with the right hand only, the second time with both hands. Please use the numbered fingering for the left hand.

Exercise 58

Exercise 59 utilizes chords built on the E-harmonic–minor scale degrees, acknowledging the D-sharp. The sharp sign is written on the staff just before the D, telling you to play the D up a half-step. Unlike the F-sharp, the sharp sign is written before each D note because D-sharp is not in the key signature of E minor. Be prepared to play the D-sharp in the first-inversion V chord (first half note chord in measure 2) and the second-inversion V chord (first half note chord in measure 4). Likewise, be sure to play the D-sharps in the left hand (second quarter note in the second and fourth measures).

Before playing **Exercise 59**, take a close look at the following table.

Table 9

Chord	Notes in the Chord	Chord Quality/Position	Fingering
1st	E–G–B	i-minor/root	thumb-E, 2nd-G, 5th-B
2nd	E–A–C**	iv-minor/2nd	thumb-E, 2nd-A, 5th-C
3rd	D#–F#–B*	V-major/1st	thumb-D#, 2nd-F#, 5th-B
4th	E–G–B	i-minor/root	thumb-E, 2nd-G, 5th-B
5th	D–G–B**	III-major/2nd	thumb-D, 2nd-G, 5th-B
6th	E–A–C**	iv-minor/2nd	thumb-E, 2nd-A, 5th-C

Chord	Notes in the Chord	Chord Quality/Position	Fingering
7th	F#–B–D#**	V-major/2nd	thumb-F#, 2nd-B, 4th-D#
8th	G–B–E*	i-minor/1st	thumb-G, 2nd-B, 5th-E

* first-inversion chords
** second-inversion chords

As you can see, **Exercise 59** also has a repeat sign. As indicated, play this exercise the first time with only the right hand. If you need to, keep repeating only the right-hand part. Once you have it worked out, then play only the left-hand part. When you have both parts worked out independently, then play the piece as written: once with the right hand only, the second time with both hands. Please use the numbered fingering for the left hand.

Exercise 59

Exercise 59 utilizes both first- and second-inversion chords. Inverted chords serve two purposes: They make the fingering easier in the chord progression, and the voices of one chord flow stepwise to the next chord. For instance, in the second measure, the first half note chord (the V chord B major) in second-inversion position has the notes D-sharp, F-sharp, and B. To get to the next chord (the root position E minor), the thumb and second finger simply move up a half-step from D-sharp to E and F-sharp to G. What's even easier is the B played by the fifth finger—it plays the top note B in the B-major chord and plays the top note B in the E-minor chord (B being the common tone in both chords).

Another example is the first-inversion B-major chord in the fourth measure with the notes F-sharp, B, and D-sharp. To get to the first-inversion E-minor chord, you simply move your thumb a half-step from F-sharp to G, and your fourth finger a half-step from D-sharp to E. The second finger stays put and plays the B in the B-major chord and then plays the same B in the E-minor chord. Here again, B is the common tone in both chords.

Playing chords only in root position is difficult and requires a lot of moving up and down the keyboard. Unlike inverted chords, when playing only root position chords in a chord progression, the changing notes from chord to chord don't flow smoothly.

Chords in the Right Hand and in the Left Hand

So far, the exercises in this chapter have dealt with playing chords with the right hand, while the left hand plays bass lines. Playing chords in the right hand is used primarily for accompaniment purposes—when accompanying a singer or solo instrumentalist. This is because the melody is being sung by the singer or played by the instrumentalist. In this scenario, the piano provides the chordal, harmonic, and rhythmic support for the melody.

Now let's put the chords in the left hand and melody in the right hand.

A pianist can play melody, harmony, and bass on the piano. The right hand can play the melody and/or chords, and the left hand can play the bass line or chords, and can also play melody.

When the piano is not in the accompaniment role, but rather in the solo role, the left hand usually plays a combination of bass lines and chords, while the right hand usually plays the melody and chords. This is the case with piano sonatas, piano concertos, and instrumental piano pieces.

In the next two exercises you will play chords in the left hand and melody in the right.

In **Exercise 60**, the left hand plays chords supporting the melody in the right hand. Take a close look at **Table 10** before playing the exercise.

Table 10

Chord	Notes in the Chord	Chord Quality/Position	Fingering
1st	D–F#–A	I-major/root	5th-D, 2nd-F#, thumb-A
2nd	D–G–B**	IV-major/2nd	5th-D, 2nd-G, thumb-B
3rd	D–F#–A	I-major/root	5th-D, 2nd-F#, thumb-A
4th	C#–E–A*	V-major/1st	4th-C#, 3rd-E, thumb-A
5th	D–F#–B*	vi-minor/1st	5th-D, 2nd-F#, thumb-B
6th	D–G–B**	IV-major/2nd	5th-D, 2nd-G, thumb-B
7th	D–G–B**	IV-major/2nd	5th-D, 2nd-G, thumb-B
8th	C#–E–A*	V-major/1st	4th-C#, 3rd-E, thumb-A
9th	D–F#–A	I-major/root	5th-D, 2nd-F#, thumb-A

* first-inversion chords

** second-inversion chords

Notice that **Exercise 60**, "Quiet Sunday," is in 3/4 time, the tempo is andante (slowly), and as the two-sharp key signature indicates, it's in the key of D major (F-sharp and C-sharp). Be sure to play all Fs and Cs sharp in both the right- and left-hand parts. As the last table indicates, most of the chords are inverted, making the harmony smooth and the fingering easy. As always, play the right- and left-hand parts separately before playing them together.

If it helps, write the left-hand chord fingering in the left-hand part.

Exercise 60

QUIET SUNDAY

Exercise 61 is written in D-harmonic minor. That's why there's a sharp sign before the C in the first-inversion V chord in the second measure. A natural sign appears before the C in the second-inversion IV chord in the third measure, canceling out the previous C-sharp. However, the C-sharp returns again in the fourth measure. Please look closely at **Table 11** before playing the exercise.

Table 11

Chord	Notes in the Chord	Chord Quality/Position	Fingering
1st	D–F–A	i-minor/root	5th-D, 2nd-F, thumb-A
2nd	D–G–Bb**	iv-minor/2nd	5th-D, 2nd-G, thumb-Bb
3rd	D–F–A	i-minor/root	5th-D, 2nd-F, thumb-A
4th	C#–E–A*	V-major/1st	4th-C#, 3rd-E, thumb-A
5th	D–F–Bb*	VI-major/1st	4th-D, 2nd-F#, thumb-Bb
6th	C–F–A**	III-major/2nd	5th-C, 2nd-F, thumb-A
7th	C#–E–A*	V-major/1st	4th-C#, 2nd-E, thumb-A
8th	D–F–A	i-minor/root	5th-D, 2nd-F, thumb-A

* first-inversion chords
** second-inversion chords

Exercise 61, "Changing C's," is in 4/4 time, and the tempo is andante (metronome marking: quarter note equals 80). This makes the tempo in this exercise slower than the tempo in **Exercise 60**. Similar to that exercise, though, most of the chords in **Exercise 61** are inverted.

In the third measure, there's a crescendo sign from *mp* to *f* followed by a decrescendo sign in the fourth measure, bringing the volume back down to *mp*. Please observe the repeat sign. This time start with only playing the left hand. Add the right hand once you have your left-hand chords in place.

Exercise 61

CHANGING C's

seven

Four-Note Chords

BOTH THE RIGHT HAND AND LEFT HAND can play four-note chords. They are based on the span of an octave, usually from the root of the chord up eight notes to its octave, along with the third and fifth of the chord in between. Four-note chords also include the first and second inversions of the root-position chords.

Making Four-Note Chords

Using some of the three-note chords (triads) from Chapter 6, let's make them four-note chords. Following **Table 12**, you can see the octave has been added for each of the chords.

Table 12

Chord	Root	Third	Fifth	Octave
C major	C	E	G	C
D major	D	F-sharp	A	D
E-flat major	E-flat	G	B-flat	E-flat
F major	F	A	C	F
G major	G	B	D	G
A major	A	C-sharp	E	A
B major	B	D-sharp	F-sharp	B

Table 13 shows the same chords in the first-inversion position.

Table 13

Chord	Third	Fifth	Root	Third
C major	E	G	C	E
D major	F-sharp	A	D	F-sharp
E-flat major	G	B-flat	E-flat	G
F major	A	C	F	A
G major	B	D	G	B

Chord	Third	Fifth	Root	Third
A major	C-sharp	E	A	C-sharp
B major	D-sharp	F-sharp	B	D-sharp

Notice that with four-note first-inversion chords, the octave occurs from the low third to the high third, eight notes above.

Here are the same chords in the second-inversion position.

Table 14

Chord	Fifth	Root	Third	Fifth
C major	G	C	E	G
D major	A	D	F-sharp	A
E-flat major	B-flat	E-flat	G	B-flat
F major	C	F	A	C
G major	D	G	B	D
A major	E	A	C-sharp	E
B major	F-sharp	B	D-sharp	F-sharp

Notice that with four-note second-inversion chords, the octave occurs from the low fifth to the high fifth, eight notes above.

Playing Four-Note Chords with the Right Hand

When playing four-note chords with the right hand, the fingering of the notes that make up the chord is consistently the same for each chord:

Root: Thumb
Third: Second finger

Fifth: Third finger
Octave: Fifth finger

The same fingering applies to first- and second-inversion chords played by the right hand. While the fingering is the same, the sequence of the notes in the chord change as follows:

First-Inversion Chords—Right Hand
Third: Thumb
Fifth: Second finger
Root: Third finger
Third: Fifth finger

Second-Inversion Chords—Right Hand
Fifth: Thumb
Root: Second finger
Third: Third finger
Fifth: Fifth finger

As you can see, when playing four-note first-inversion chords with the right hand, there's an octave from the third played by the thumb to the third played by the fifth finger, eight notes above. When playing four-note second-inversion chords, an octave occurs from the fifth of the chord to the fifth, eight notes above.

Playing Four-Note Chords with the Left Hand

When playing four-note chords with the left hand, the fingering of the notes that make up the chord is also consistently the same for each chord:

Root: Fifth finger
Third: Third finger
Fifth: Second finger
Octave: Thumb

The same fingering applies to first- and second-inversion chords played by the left hand. While the fingering is the same, the sequence of the notes in the chord changes as follows:

First-Inversion Chords—Left Hand
Third: Fifth finger
Fifth: Third finger
Root: Second finger
Third: Thumb

Second-Inversion Chords—Left Hand
Fifth: Fifth finger
Fifth: Fifth finger
Third: Second finger
Fifth: Thumb

Here again, when playing four-note first-inversion chords with the left hand, there's an octave from the third played by the fifth finger to the third played by the thumb, eight notes above. When playing four-note second-inversion chords, an octave occurs from the fifth of the chord to the fifth, eight notes above.

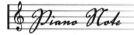

As you become more experienced, you may start to use your piano's pedals: the *sustain* pedal is on the right, and the *damper* pedal is on the left). The sustain pedal releases the damper pads, allowing the strings to resonate longer until the sounds naturally dissipate, or until you take your foot off the pedal. The damper (also known as *soft*) pedal causes the hammers to make less sound when hitting the strings. The middle pedal found on many pianos, called the *sostenuto* pedal, is rarely used; it has the effect of sustaining the first chord in a series, or common notes between chords.

Four-Note Chord Exercises

In **Exercise 62**, you will play four-note chords with your right hand. Please use the same fingering for each chord: root–thumb; third–second finger; fifth–third finger; octave–fifth finger.

Exercise 62

In this exercise, all of the chords are major chords: C major, D major, and E-flat major. As a group, these chords don't belong to one specific key signature. Therefore, no key signature is written on the staff. Generally speaking, when there isn't a sharp or flat key signature that means the music is in the key of C major or A minor. However, this is not the case here because we are using major chords from more than one key signature, and we're even mixing sharp (the D-major chord) and flat (the E-flat–major chord) major chords together. Be sure to acknowledge the F-sharp in the D-major chord, and the E- and B-flats in the E-flat–major chord.

In **Exercise 63**, a rhythmic bass line is added to the same chord progression. This bass line, played by the left-hand thumb, stays on the C note, an octave below middle C. As you can see, there is a curved line called a tie, which ties together the first quarter note with the first eighth note in the second beat of measures 1, 2, 3, and 4. The tie means the first eighth note is heard but not played because it is tied to the quarter note. But you do play the second eighth note, which is the subdivision of the second beat in the measure. To get a feel for the tied rhythm played by the left hand, count out loud the following:

ONE	two	**AND**	**THREE**	four
(Quarter	eighth	**eighth**	**half**	**)**

The above numbers in bold and the corresponding note values represent the beats and notes to play with the left hand in **Exercise 63**. When counting out loud, put an emphasis on *one, and,* and *three*. As you recall, two eighth notes equal one quarter note. A subdivision is simply dividing a single quarter beat into two eighth beats.

Harmonically, the moving right-hand chords over the repeated C in the bass creates tension in measures 2, 3, and 4, and then resolves in the fifth measure with the left hand playing the root of the C-major chord, doubled down an octave. The harmonic tension in measures 2, 3, and 4 is created because the bass note C is not a note within the triadic structure of the D and E-flat chords. As a reminder, the triadic structure of a chord is comprised of the root, third, and fifth.

As indicated, the right-hand chords have their letter names written above each chord.

Exercise 63

Another name for a tied rhythm is a dotted rhythm. The value of a dotted note is equal to the note's value plus half its value. For example, a dotted quarter note equals one quarter beat plus a half beat, or in other words, a beat and a half. As you can see in **Exercise 63**, the quarter note tied to the eighth note equals a beat and a half. So another way of writing the exact same rhythm is to use a dotted quarter note followed by a single eighth note, instead of a quarter note tied to an eighth note. See **Exercise 64**.

Exercise 64

Now let's move on to playing four-note chords with the left hand.

In **Exercise 65**, the left hand plays the following four-note chords: C major, D major, and E major (not E-flat major). Please be sure to acknowledge the sharps in the D- and E-major chords. The left-hand fingering of all of the chords in this exercise is: root–fifth finger; third–third finger; fifth–second finger; octave–thumb. Also notice that the last chord (E major) played in measure 7 is tied to the same chord in measure 8. Play the E-major chord in measure 7, keep it held down, and let it sustain through the end of measure 8.

Exercise 65

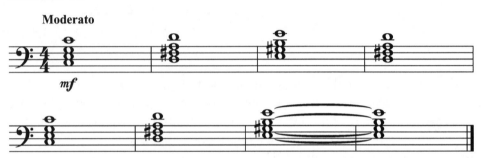

As you can see in the next exercise, a dotted, or tied, rhythm is played by the right hand. The rhythm is written in two different ways: a quarter note tied to an eighth note (measures 1 and 4) and a dotted quarter note (measures 2, 3, 5, and 6). The rhythm in measures 1 through 6 is exactly the same, and sounds the same, even though the rhythm is written in two different ways.

This dotted rhythm is the same rhythm that the left hand played in **Exercises 63 and 64**, with one exception: The rhythm is different in the seventh measure. The rhythm of the third and fourth beats in the seventh measure is also a tied (dotted) rhythm (the fourth beat is tied to the preceding quarter note; the and of the fourth beat, the second eighth note, is played). It's exactly the same rhythm as the first two beats in the measure.

Let's look at the harmonic relationship between the right-hand melody and left-hand chords in **Exercise 66**. The repeated E note played by the right hand is harmonically consonant (resolved) with the chords played by the left hand in measures 1, 3, 5, 7, and 8. This is because the note E is also the third in the C-major chord and the root and octave in the E-major chord. Because both the C- and E-major chords have the note E in their triadic

116

structure, E is referred to as the common tone between the two chords. In measures 2, 4, and 6, the E note in the right hand creates some tension against the D chord because the E note is not a pitch that makes up the D-major triad.

Exercise 66

Breaking It Down

Exercise 67, "Safe and Sound?", is comprised of a simple melody in the right hand and moving four-note chords in the left hand. It's the moving harmony of the chords juxtaposed to the simple melody that makes this exercise interesting.

Table 15 identifies the quality, position, and fingering of the chords used in **Exercise 67**.

Table 15

Measure	Notes in the Chord	Quality/Position	Fingering
1	Eb–G–Bb–Eb	I-major/root	5th-Eb, 3rd-G, 2nd-Bb, thumb-Eb
2	Eb–G–Bb–D	I-major 7th/root	5th-Eb, 3rd-G, 2nd-Bb, thumb-D
3	C–Eb–G–C	vi-minor/root	5th-C, 3rd-Eb, 2nd-G, thumb-C
4	C–Eb–Ab–C*	IV-major/1st	5th-C, 3rd-Eb, 2nd-Ab, thumb-C
5	C–F–Ab–C**	ii-minor/2nd	5th-C, 3rd-F, 2nd-Ab, thumb-C
6	Db–F–Ab–Db^	VII-major/root	5th-Db, 3rd-F, 2nd-Ab, thumb-Db
7	D–F–Bb–D*	V-major/1st	5th-D, 3rd-F, 2nd-Bb, thumb-D
8	Eb–G–Bb–Eb	I-major/root	5th-Eb, 3rd-G, 2nd-Bb, thumb-Eb

* first-inversion chords

** second-inversion chords

^ lowered seventh chord

There are two new chords introduced in **Exercise 67**. In the second measure, the chord is E-flat–major seventh. It's called a major seventh chord because the distance between the root E-flat and D is an interval of a major seventh. This interval is added on to the E-flat major triad. In the sixth measure, the chord is D-flat major. This is an altered chord because in the key of E-flat major, the seventh scale degree is D-natural, not D-flat. Even though D-flat is not in the key of E-flat major, this chord works well because the D-flat is a stepwise, passing tone from C to D. Additionally, F minor and D-flat major have two common tones: F and A-flat.

While all the notes of the chords provide harmony for the melody, take a look at the top note in each chord. The top notes of the chords measure by measure are: E-flat, D, C, C, C, D-flat, D-natural, and E-flat. This top harmonic voice moves smoothly in a stepwise motion while the other notes (voices) in the chord move beneath it. This top note is also strong harmonically because it is doubled an octave lower throughout the chord progression with the exception of the second measure. When notes are doubled and played in octaves, their sounds dominate the other notes in the chord.

Play only the left-hand chords several times before adding the right-hand melody. In doing so, you will discover common tones among the chords and smooth harmonic changes by playing inversions. As indicated, **Exercise 67** is in the key of E-flat major. Be sure to play all the flats as indicated in the key signature.

Exercise 67

SAFE and SOUND?

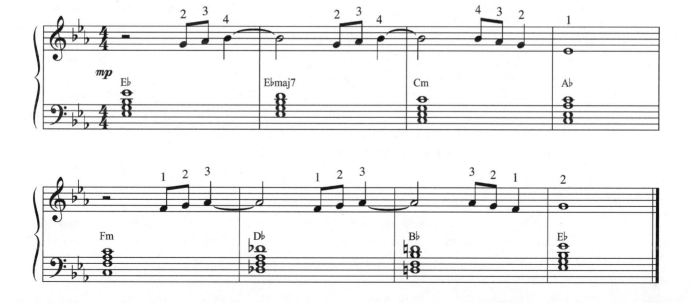

Pulling Everything Together

Exercise 68, "Underground," is in 6/8 time. That means that there are six eighth notes, or the equivalent thereof, per measure. When counting the eighth notes, count 1-2-3, 2-2-3 for each measure, with an accent on the first eighth note in each group of three. This gives the 6/8 time signature a two-beat feel with three eighth-note subdivisions per beat. When playing this piece with a two-beat feel, the tempo is largo, which is slow. Keep in mind that there are two sets of three even eighth notes per beat.

Because **Exercise 68** is in the key of D-harmonic minor, the seventh scale degree is C-sharp. As indicated in measures 4 and 8, the C-sharp makes the V chord A major. The dotted quarter note chords equal three eighth notes (two eighth notes in a quarter plus the dot equals half the value of a quarter note, which is an eighth). The dotted half note chords equal two dotted quarter notes or six eighth notes. The left hand plays four-note chords throughout the piece except for the very last D-minor chord, which is a three-note chord. This occurs because the right hand plays the top note D. The fingering of the chords in the left hand is the same throughout: fifth finger, third finger, second finger, and thumb, except for the last chord, played with the fifth finger, third finger, and second finger. The G-minor chord in measures 2, 3, 6, and 7 are second inversions, starting with the fifth of the chord D, followed by G, B-flat, and D. The A chord in measures 4 and 8 are first inversions, starting with the third of the chord C-sharp, followed by E, A, and C-sharp.

Play only the left-hand chords several times. Take time, practice the chords, listen to the four voices that make up the chord and how the voices change from chord to chord. You'll hear the common tone (D) between D minor and G minor, and how the first-inversion A chord makes a smooth harmonic progression to D minor.

Once you have the chords worked out comfortably with your left hand, play only the melody with your right hand. Notice how measures 5, 6, and 7 are exactly the same as measures 1, 2, and 3.

And please observe the D-minor key signature and play all Bs flat.

Piano Note

Before playing any piece of music, it's always best to analyze all of the parts: the key signature, tempo/metronome marking, time signature, the right-hand part, the melody, the left-hand part, the harmony, the fingering, the rhythm, and dynamic markings. The vast majority of piano pieces don't have the right- and left-hand fingering written in the part. So, you have to go through the piece and determine which fingers to use for each hand.

Exercise 68

UNDERGROUND

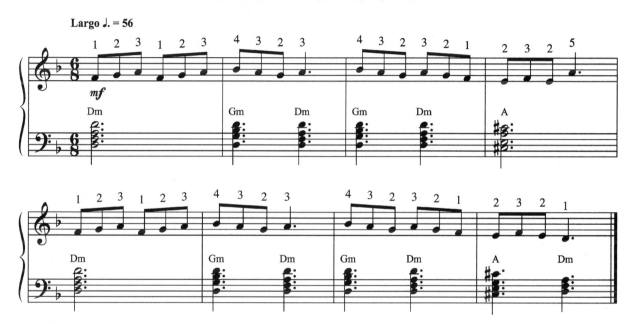

eight

**More Advanced
Chords and
Techniques**

YES, THIS IS STILL the only *basic* piano instruction book you'll ever need. In this chapter, though, you'll get an introduction to some concepts that are a little more advanced. We'll start with the various types of seventh chords and how to construct them. You'll then get a brief introduction to other types of chords and to the art of improvisation—all things you can delve into more deeply as you continue your piano studies.

Major Sevenths

Major seventh chords are consonant. They are built on major key scale degrees. In major key scales, the seventh scale degree is a half-step below the octave.

As you know, chords are comprised of thirds: a major third and a minor third equal a major triad; a minor third and a major third equal a minor triad. Going up another third from the fifth of a chord gives us the seventh. For example, the notes in a C-major chord are C (root), E (third), and G (fifth). A major third above G is B. When you stack up the thirds in a C-major seventh chord you have: C, E, G, B (C to E is a major third, E to G is a minor third, and G to B is a major third). So the formula for all major seventh chords is a sequence of a major third, minor third, and major third.

Table 16 shows you the notes and consecutive thirds in major seventh chords.

Table 16

Chord	Root	Third	Fifth	Seventh
D-major 7th	D	F-sharp	A	C-sharp
F-major 7th	F	A	C	E
G-major 7th	G	B	D	F-sharp
A-major 7th	A	C-sharp	E	G-sharp
B-major 7th	B	D-sharp	F-sharp	A-sharp

In keeping with the major seventh formula, notice that the interval from the root to the third with all of the chords is a major third, from the third to the fifth is a minor third, and from the fifth to the seventh is a major third.

When playing the D-, G-, A-, and B-major seventh chords in the above table with the right hand, the fingering is:

Root: Thumb
Third: Second finger
Fifth: Third finger
Seventh: Fourth finger

The fingering is slightly different for the F-major seventh chord:

Root: Thumb
Third: Second finger
Fifth: Third finger
Seventh: Fifth finger

The difference in the fingering is because when the seventh in a major seventh chord is located on a black key, the fourth finger (which is longer than the fifth finger) can easily reach the black key. However, when the seventh in a major seventh chord is located on a white key, the fifth finger is a better choice.

In **Exercise 69**, play the major seventh chords in the above table with your right hand.

Exercise 69: Major seventh chords

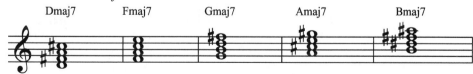

When playing the chords with your left hand, the fingering is:

Root: Fifth finger
Third: Third finger
Fifth: Second finger
Seventh: Thumb

This left-hand fingering applies to all major seventh chords, black and white keys alike. In **Exercise 70**, play the major seventh chords in the table on p. 124 with your left hand.

Exercise 70: Major seventh chords

Dmaj7   Fmaj7   Gmaj7   Amaj7   Bmaj7

In **Exercise 71** you're going to build major seventh chords following the major third, minor third, major third formula. Build up from the roots starting with middle C. (Reminder: The major seventh is a half-step below the octave.)

Exercise 71: Construcing major seventh chords

	Root	Third	Fifth	Seventh
C				
E-flat				
F-sharp				
A				
B-flat				

Now that you have constructed the chords, play them with your right hand in **Exercise 72**.

Exercise 72: Major seventh chords

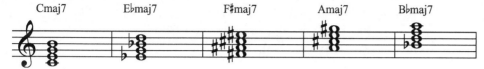

Minor Seventh Chords

The following minor seventh chords are built on natural minor scale degrees. The seventh scale degree in natural minor scales is a whole step below the octave.

The stacking up of thirds for natural minor seventh chords follows this formula: minor third, major third, and minor third. **Table 17** shows you the notes and consecutive thirds in natural minor seventh chords.

Table 17

Chord	Root	Third	Fifth	Seventh
C-minor 7th	C	E-flat	G	B-flat*
D-minor 7th	D	F	A	C
E-minor 7th	E	G	B	D
F-minor 7th	F	A-flat	C	E-flat*
G-minor 7th	G	B-flat	D	F
A-minor 7th	A	C	E	G
B-minor 7th	B	D	F-sharp	A

* The sevenths that are on black keys are played using the fourth finger.

Note that all of the chords in the above table follow the natural minor seventh formula—from the root to the third is a minor third, from the third to the fifth is a major third, and from the fifth to the seventh is a minor third.

When playing minor seventh chords with the right hand, the fingering is the same as playing major seventh chords. As indicated with one asterisk in **Table 17**, the sevenths that are on black keys are played using the fourth finger. All of the other sevenths, which are on white keys, are played using the fifth finger.

In **Exercise 73**, play the chords in the last table with your right hand.

Exercise 73: Minor seventh chords

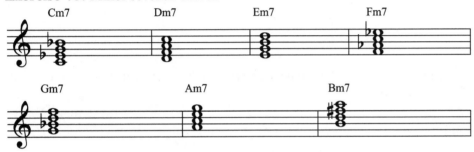

When playing minor seventh chords with the left hand, the fingering is the same as playing major seventh chords. In **Exercise 74**, play the minor seventh chords in **Table 17** with your left hand.

Exercise 74: Minor seventh chords

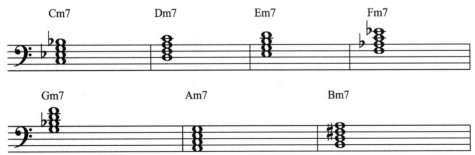

In **Exercise 75**, build natural minor seventh chords following the minor third, major third, minor third formula. Start with the root, E-flat. (Reminder: The minor seventh is a whole step below the octave.)

Exercise 75: Constructing Minor Seventh Chords

	Root	Third	Fifth	Seventh
E-flat				
F-sharp				
A				
B-flat				

Now that you have constructed the chords, play them with your right hand in **Exercise 76**.

Exercise 76: Minor seventh chords

Harmonic Minor Sevenths

Minor seventh chords with an interval of a major seventh from the root to the seventh are built on harmonic minor scale degrees. The seventh scale degree in harmonic minor scales is a half-step below the octave.

The stacking up of thirds for harmonic minor seventh chords follows this formula: minor third, major third, and major third. Rather than calling them harmonic minor seventh chords, they are commonly referred to as minor chords with a raised seventh—raised because the seventh is a half-step higher than the natural minor seventh. For example, the notes in a G-minor seventh chord are G, B-flat, D, and F. In a G minor with a raised seventh, the notes are: G, B-flat, D, and F-sharp. The shorthand version chord symbol for harmonic minor chords is Gm+7. The "+" is shorthand for raised.

The difference between major seventh chords and minor chords with a raised seventh is only one pitch: the third of the chord. For example, the notes in a C-major seventh chord are C, E, G, and B. The notes in a C minor with a raised seventh are C, E-flat, G, and B. The simple change of a lowered half-step with the third of the chord makes a big difference in the way these two chords sound.

To illustrate this difference, alternate playing between C-major seventh and C minor with a raised seventh. Use middle C as the root of both chords.

Dominant Seventh Chords

The seventh chords we have covered so far are all built on the first scale degree—the root. Dominant seventh chords are built on the fifth scale degree—the dominant.

In the key of C major, the dominant seventh is G7. This chord is comprised of the G-major triad plus a minor seventh interval from the root G up to F. The notes in the G7 chord are G, B, D, and F. Dominant seventh chords want to resolve to the root. When playing in a major key, C major for instance, the G7 also has a sense of resolution by going to the vi chord, A minor. The formula for all dominant seventh chords is a sequence of a major third, minor third, and minor third.

Dominant seventh chords are also used in harmonic minor keys. For example, in the key of E-harmonic minor, the V chord is B major. B major becomes B7 by adding the note A. The notes in the B7 chord are B, D-sharp, F-sharp, and A.

In the next exercise, build dominant seventh chords following the major third, minor third, minor third formula. Start with the root E, two whole steps above middle C. (Reminder: The minor seventh is a whole step below the octave.)

Exercise 77: Constructing Dominant Seventh Chords

	Root	Third	Fifth	Seventh
E				
F				
G				
A				
B-flat				
C				

When you have constructed the dominant seventh chords in **Exercise 77**, play them with your right hand in **Exercise 78**.

Exercise 78: Dominant seventh chords

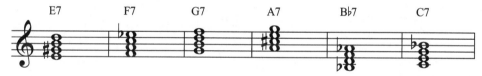

Seventh-Chord Inversions

Seventh chords can be inverted to first, second, or third positions. With a first-inversion, E-dominant seventh chord, the notes are G-sharp, B, D, and E. In a second-inversion, C-major seventh, the notes are G, B, C, and E. The first note in a third-inversion chord is the seventh. For example, the notes in an F-major seventh third-inversion chord are E, F, A, and C.

The following table shows seventh chords in third-inversion positions.

Table 18

Chord	Seventh	Root	Third	Fifth
C-minor 7th	B-flat	C	E-flat	G
D-major 7th	C-sharp	D	F-sharp	A
E-dominant 7th	D	E	G-sharp	B
F-minor 7th	E-flat	F	A-flat	C
G-major 7th	F-sharp	G	B	D
A-minor +7th	G-sharp	A	C	E
B-major 7th	A-sharp	B	D-sharp	F-sharp

Play the chords in the above table with your right hand in **Exercise 79**. The fingering is the same for all of the chords:

Seventh: Thumb
Root: Second finger
Third: Third finger
Fifth: Fifth finger

Exercise 79: Third-inversion seventh chords

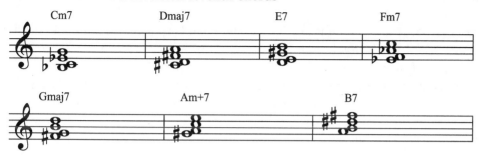

Exercise 80 uses a variety of seventh chords in the right hand over a rhythmic bass line. **Table 19** identifies the chord qualities and their positions.

Table 19

Measure	Chord	Notes	Quality	Position
1	C-major 7th*	E–G–B	I-major 7th	1st inversion
2	F-major 7th	E–F–A–C	IV-major 7th	3rd inversion
3	E major**	E–G#–B	V-dominant	root position
4	A minor	E–A–C	iv-minor	2nd inversion
5	F-major 7th*	E–A–C	IV-major	3rd inversion
6	E-dominant 7th**	E–G#–B–D	V-dominant 7th	root position
7	A minor	E–A–C	iv-minor	2nd inversion
8	A minor	E–A–C–E	iv-minor	2nd inversion

* root in bass
** borrowed dominant

Up until now, you have been playing closed-position chords. In the next exercise you will be playing two open-position chords.

Looking at the very first chord (C-major seventh), it looks like the right hand is playing an E-minor chord. But when you add the root of the chord, C, played by the bass, the E-minor chord becomes a C-major seventh chord. Likewise, in measure 5, the root of the F-major seventh chord is played by the bass. The voicings of the C-major seventh and F-major seventh chords are good examples of open-position chords, where the notes that make up the chord are played in different octaves. All other chords in **Exercise 80** are closed-position chords.

As indicated with two asterisks in **Table 19**, the E-major and E-dominant seventh chords are borrowed dominants from the key of A minor. In the key of C major, the iii chord is minor. By making it major, it becomes the V chord in the key of A minor. In doing so, we move from the key of C major to A minor. **Exercise 80** starts in the key of C major, but after two measures, transposes to the key of A minor and stays in that key for the remainder of the piece.

In the left-hand part, notice the dotted rhythm on the first two beats of every measure except for the last measure. The rhythm of the bass part in measure 1 is repeated in measures 3, 4, 6, and 7. A variation of this rhythm takes place on the fourth beat in measures 2 and 5.

There is a common tone among all of the chords in this exercise. One note is played in the same position throughout the chord progression. It's the note E, which is the first note in every chord played by the thumb in the right hand.

Play only the right-hand chords several times. Then play only the left-hand bass part several times. When you're ready, play with both hands together. You'll notice when you add the bass part to the chords in measures 1, 2, and 5 how significantly the sound of the harmony changes.

MOVING ON

Other Types of Chords

Now that you have added seventh chords to your repertoire, we'll just briefly describe the other types of chords that you will learn more about as you study the piano further.

Ninth Chords

An octave is eight notes above any given pitch. A whole step above an octave is a ninth. For example, starting with the root G, eight notes above is the octave G, a whole step above the octave G is A, which is the ninth. Ninths can be added to all types of major chords and all minor chords, including seventh chords.

There are also flat ninth chords. The flat ninth chord is built on a dominant seventh chord.

It's flat because the ninth is lowered a half-step. Using an F-dominant seventh chord as an example, by adding a G-flat, it becomes a flat ninth chord. The notes in the chord are F, A, C, E-flat, and G-flat. The abbreviated chord symbol for flat ninth chords is F7♭9. Flat ninth chords are very dissonant.

Suspended Chords

Suspended chords include the second and fourth scale degrees in major and minor chords. The written shorthand for suspended chords is *sus*. They are called suspended chords because the suspended pitch (note) wants to resolve to either the root, third, or fifth of the chord. For example, a C sus2 chord contains the second scale degree D. The D can resolve to either C (the root) or E (the third). A C sus4 chord contains the fourth scale degree F. The F can resolve to E (the third) or G (the fifth). The second (D) resolves by either going up a whole step to E or down a whole step to the root; the fourth (F) resolves by moving down a half-step to E or up a whole step to G.

Diminished Chords

We learned in Chapter 6 that chords built on the seventh scale degree in major keys are diminished chords. Diminished chords are a half-step smaller than minor chords. For example, the two third intervals that make up a G-minor chord are a minor third (from G to B-flat) and a major third (from B-flat to D). By lowering the major third a half-step and making it a minor third, we have two minor thirds that equal a diminished chord. The notes in a G-diminished chord are G, B-flat, and D-flat.

Adding to the two minor third triads that make up a diminished chord (by adding another minor third on top of the fifth), we get a diminished seventh chord. Using the G-diminished triad, a minor third above the fifth is F-flat.

Diminished chords are dissonant and want to resolve. The shorthand for writing diminished chords is *dim.* (G dim.7).

Augmented Chords

You may recall that the III chord built on a harmonic minor scale is an augmented chord. *Augment* means to make larger. Augmented chords are a half-step larger than a major triad. For example, the two third intervals that make up a D-major chord are a major third (from D to F-sharp) and a minor third (from F-sharp to A). By raising the minor third a half-step and making it a major third, we have two major thirds that equal an augmented chord. The notes in a D-augmented chord are D, F-sharp, and A-sharp.

Augmented chords are also dissonant chords that want to resolve. The shorthand for writing augmented chords is *aug.* (A aug).

Arpeggio Chords (Broken Chords)

In contrast to the way you have been playing chords thus far, another way of playing chords is to arpeggiate, or break up, the notes that make up the chord and play each note individually. The Italian word *arpeggio* means "harp-like." Arpeggio chords can be played by either the right hand or the left hand.

Piano Note

Piano pieces can be written in a specific style or left open for your own stylistic adaptation. Musical styles cover a wide range, including baroque, classical, romantic, impressionistic, ragtime, stride, abstract, jazz, bebop, boogie-woogie, rhythm and blues, country, gospel, rock and roll, show tunes (Broadway musicals), pop, soul, disco, funk, reggae, and New Age. If specified, try to play the piece in the style it's written in.

Abbreviated Chord Symbols

Every chord has a symbol representing its quality. The following list is an example of chords, their quality, and their corresponding symbol.

Chord/Quality	Symbol
C major	C*
D-major seventh	Dmaj.7
E-dominant seventh	E7**
F minor	Fm
G-minor seventh	Gm7
A-flat–major ninth	A♭9
A-minor ninth	Am9
B-suspended second	Bsus2
C-suspended fourth	Csus4
D diminished	Ddim.
E-flat–diminished seventh	E♭dim.7
F augmented	Faug.
B-flat minor, raised seventh	B♭min+7
C-dominant seventh, flat nine	C7♭9

*: A letter name without any abbreviations or numbers represents a major chord.

**: A letter name followed by a seven represents a dominant seventh chord.

Some piano music has the melody, harmony (chords), and bass line written out in fine detail. This is the case with classical pieces. With jazz, pop, and rock piano music, sometimes the specific harmony is not written. Instead, chord symbols are written above the melody. The sequence of chords is called a chord progression.

Playing a chord chart requires a lot of keyboard experience and the ability to construct chords based on chord symbols. The pianist has to know all of the notes that belong in the chord and which position to play the chord: root, first inversion, second inversion, or third inversion.

The first step in this process is to go through the entire chord progression and figure out the fingering and positions of the chords with the left hand. Once that is accomplished, then add the melody with the right hand.

Improvisation

Some chord charts have no written melody or harmony at all. The rhythm is indicated by slanted slash marks. This type of chord chart is used primarily by pianists who accompany singers or solo instrumentalists. The singer or instrumentalist sings or plays the melody while the pianist provides the chordal (harmonic) rhythmic accompaniment. In order to do this successfully, it usually requires years of keyboard experience and working with other musicians—soloists and singers alike. It also requires the ability to improvise or fill in. A keyboard player in a band typically plays solos. When playing from a chord chart that has no written notes to play, the pianist has to improvise; in other words, the pianist has to make up solos on the spot.

Improvisation is a very special skill. Some pianists can acquire and develop this skill. Other pianists have difficulty improvising and prefer to play from much more detailed written music. Playing from chord charts is certainly for the advanced keyboard player who knows how to improvise.

appendix

The Only Piano Quiz
You'll Ever Need
to Take
(in This Book)

NOW THAT YOU'VE made it through the entire book (if not, go back and keep going!), this quiz will help you to evaluate how well you've absorbed what you've learned. The questions generally follow the order of the book's chapters, and, as with the book itself, they get somewhat harder as they go along. If you have trouble with a series of questions, review the part of the book that covers those topics until the concepts become more familiar. Good luck!

1. Put the following types of piano in order from smallest to largest:

   _____ baby grand   _____ console   _____ concert grand

   _____ spinet   _____ upright   _____ studio

2. How often should you tune an acoustic piano? A digital piano?

   _____

For questions 3–9, examine Exercise 2 from Chapter 2, reproduced below.

3. How many bars are there in Exercise 2?
4. How many notes are there in bar 3?
5. What kinds of notes are in the exercise?
6. How many beats are there per measure?
7. What is the name of the clef?
8. What do the numbers above the notes represent?
9. What is the name of the zigzag line in measure 4, and how many beats is it equal to?
10. In musical terms, what is the English meaning of the following Italian terms?

    _____ a. moderato   d. adagio

    _____ b. allegro   e. crescendo

    _____ c. forte   f. andante

11. What are the letter names of the lines on a staff from bottom to top when using a treble clef? What are the letter names of the spaces from bottom to top?

12. What are the letter names of the lines on a staff from *top to bottom* when using a bass clef? What are the letter names of the spaces from top to bottom?

13. Where is middle C located when using the bass clef?

14. What do flats do to a note? What do sharps do?

15. How many sharps does the key of C major have? What is its relative minor?

16. What is the "whole step/half step" pattern for all major keys, beginning with the root? What is the pattern for all minor keys?

17. Which key signatures have one sharp? Which have two sharps?

18. What does "quarter note equals 108" mean?

19. What does a dotted half note equal?

20. Flat key signatures follow what kind of circle?

21. How many flats does the key of C minor have?

22. What's another word for a three-note chord?

23. How many intervals are there in a major chord? What type are they?

24. What types of intervals comprise minor chords?

25. What note is a fifth above A-flat?

26. What note is a major third above C-sharp?

27. What is the third chord in the key of C major?

28. What is a root-position chord? A first-inversion chord? A second-inversion chord?

29. What chord is diminished in the key of E-natural minor?

30. What are four-note chords based on?

31. What happens when notes are tied together?

32. C-major and E-major chords have a common tone. What is it?

33. What is the formula for building major seventh chords?

34. What are the notes in a root-position, A-flat–major seventh chord?

35. What's another word for broken chords?

Answers

1. Spinet, console, studio, upright, baby grand, concert grand.
2. Acoustic pianos should be tuned at least once a year, and in some cases every six months. Digital pianos, which have no strings, never need to be tuned.
3. Four.
4. Four.
5. Quarter notes.
6. Four.
7. Treble clef; also called a G clef.
8. Fingering indications for the first three fingers of the right hand.
9. A quarter rest; one beat.
10. a. Moderately (playing not too fast or too slow); b. Fast; c. Loudly; d. Slowly; e. Gradually play louder; f. Moderately slow.
11. The lines are E, G, B, D, F; and the spaces are F, A, C, E.
12. The lines are A, F, D, B, G; and the spaces are G, E, C, A.
13. One ledger line above the staff.
14. Flats lower the pitch down a half-step, while sharps raise it a half-step.
15. It has no sharps (or flats); its relative minor is A minor.
16. For major keys: whole/whole/half/whole/whole/whole/half. For minor keys: whole/half/whole/whole/half/whole/whole.
17. G major and E minor have one sharp; D major and B minor have two.
18. It is a metronome marking, which tells you the rate of speed of the quarter note in a piece of music. "108" indicates a speed of 108 beats per minute.
19. Three quarter beats.
20. A circle of fourths.
21. Three.
22. Triad.
23. Two—a major third followed by a minor third.

24. A minor third followed by a major third.
25. E-flat.
26. E-sharp.
27. E minor.
28. A root-position chord is one that starts with the root followed by the third and fifth. A first-inversion chord is one that starts with the third followed by the fifth and root. A second-inversion chord is one that starts with the fifth followed by the root and third.
29. The ii chord: F-sharp diminished.
30. The span of an octave.
31. You play their combined value.
32. E.
33. From the root of a chord, build a major third (root to third), minor third (third to fifth), and a major third (fifth to seventh).
34. A-flat, C, E-flat, G.
35. Arpeggio chords.

Index